Praise for
The Life Blueprint Process

Life Blueprint changed my views, my vantage point,
and my ability to adapt. We are often unable to change
our circumstances, but we can always change our mindset.
I cannot thank Nicole enough for changing my perspective
and my attitude as I welcome in a new year with open arms!

M., Executive, New York City, US

In such a fast-paced world, we rarely afford ourselves
a moment to simply evaluate where we are and where
we want to be. The Life Blueprint process helped me put
into perspective my vision for my career and my future,
allowing me to understand how to incorporate my interests,
my skills, and my values into my version of success.

J., Post-Grad Student, London, UK

....

The Life Blueprint Workshop was the most valuable investment I've made on focusing my time to think about my personal priorities and life goals. The outcome of the process has helped me, on a daily basis, be on the right path to achieve my goals. I'm so grateful for Nicole and her masterful teaching and practical framework.

M., VP of a Major Bank, Global
(just transitioned to being a digital nomad)

....

The Life Blueprint process enabled me to broaden my lens and think critically about the steps I can take to accomplish my goals, all while maximizing enjoyment through this crazy journey called Life. That is my way of measuring success!

C., Founder, Toronto, Canada

....

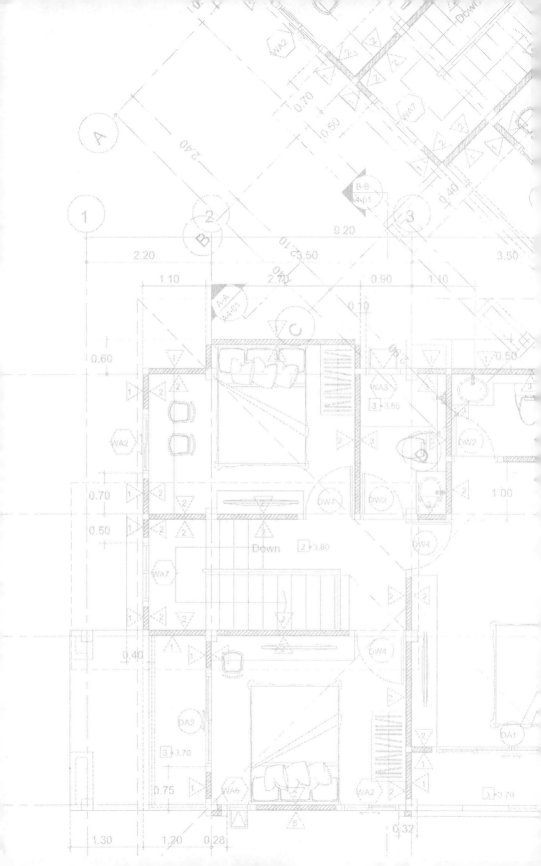

LIFE
BLUEPRINT

*A step-by-step guide
for creating
an extraordinary life*

NICOLE GALLUCCI

LIFE BLUEPRINT

2023 YGTMedia Co. Press Trade Paperback Edition.

Copyright © 2023 Nicole Gallucci

Published in Canada, for Global Distribution by YGTMedia Co.

www.ygtmedia.co

For more information email: publishing@ygtmedia.co

ISBN trade paperback: 978-1-998754-46-5

To order additional copies of this book: publishing@ygtmedia.co

AUTHOR'S NOTE: My intent is to educate and inspire you. I am not a medical doctor or therapist and am not providing medical advice. If you are suffering or struggling with a physical or mental health issue, then please seek counsel from a medical expert. I am a seasoned business professional with a myriad of experience, and it is from that context that I have developed the Life Blueprint methodology and am sharing it with you.

To my children,
You are my greatest teachers
and my unequivocal reason for being.
I love you more than life itself.

To You,
This book is for anyone at a crossroads
or wondering if there is more.
This book is for those who have goals and dreams they
no longer want to put aside due to life's demands.
This book is for everyone wanting a methodology
for creating an extraordinary life!
Now is the time to design the plans and build
the life you want.
If not now, when?

Contents

Preface

Are you pondering life?
Me too.

What is the meaning of life?
How do we live a meaningful life?
When do we do this?
How do we do this?

In 1945, Viktor E. Frankl wrote *Man's Search for Meaning*, which remains today one of the premier books on evaluating and creating meaningful lives. With fierce determination, Frankl wrote the book and never intended or expected it, that it would be his most remarkable work and still so relevant today. His intent was to "convey to the reader by way of concrete example that life holds a potential meaning under any conditions, even the most miserable ones." This book, *Life Blueprint,* is my "meaning." My conditions are far from miserable or even remotely comparable to Frankl's experience in the Auschwitz concentration camps. Rather, my book is the result of a first-world life impacted by childhood traumas, the abandonment by great loves, the loss of precious lives, corruption, the threat of violence, reputational misjudgment and misunderstanding, extreme bliss and joy, and the juxtaposition of it all. Some of these, I am sure you can also relate to. The individual and cumulative impact of many events, some very significant and others, part of living and working, have led me to contemplate with great intensity the positives and challenges of living.

I have survived and thrived in spite of facing many adversities. As a result, I feel as though it is incumbent upon me to share learnings that may make the lives of others easier. I am publishing this work at an age and stage where and when I have credibility. To have done it sooner would have been, in my opinion, folly. There is a wisdom in life experiences that can only be shared when you experience life. And I am all about experience—sometimes to a fault (I am laughing at myself as I type this). I live trying new things, seeking adventures, spontaneously pursuing opportunities, walking around hidden corners, only to be delighted, rarely dismayed. I live out of my comfort zone in the hopes that others will do the same according to their own comfort level.

My mission is to inspire and have an impact. My intent is that in doing so, others can also have an impact. And in the process, we all live more fully, more happily, and by positive default, the world becomes a better place.

While Frankl's book beckons us to have meaning, some of us need a step-by-step process to achieve that meaning, and in my case, inspire and have an impact. We are reminded daily of many who have overcome great tragedy, loss, and incomprehensible atrocities and have gone on to do great things—I am not one of those people. I am an ordinary soul seeking to live an extraordinary life. A white, North American woman, I am greatly thankful that I have only read about atrocities. I make this point because I think this may be the case for many of us. Though we live in a "safe" place, relatively speaking, we want more or different or extraordinary. And that is okay. Don't feel bad for wanting more; we are all worthy of extraordinary regardless of our beginnings and/or stories.

It is the seeking of more, better, extraordinary that has fueled our need for self-help books, coaches, courses, workshops, and more. Their intent is to offer a guiding hand to help us interpret these desires and then create a path to achieve them. And trust me when I say I have been one of these seekers. I have put out my hand in the hopes it will be grabbed by a guide a million times. Obviously, this is an overstatement, but I want you to know I have searched because I was in great need and there was not one holistic, integrated approach for tackling and/or optimizing life. For managing all the ebbs and flows and coming out the other side. Where all the books and courses and coaches fell short was in providing a simple, easy-to-follow, end-to-end solution for creating a life of meaning. **This book, *Life Blueprint*, is the solution to this challenging life issue. It saved my life and helped me achieve my goals and dreams**. The Life Blueprint process was my breakthrough in creating a holistic plan for a life of meaning for myself. It helped me clarify what truly matters to me and how I want to show up every day in the hopes of making a valuable impact, thus living fully for myself and serving others in the process. Others noticed the shift in me and asked me to share what I was doing, to help them. And so, I began to share the process. To date, thousands have worked through it in search of extraordinary. Our cumulative positive and extraordinary results are the reason my methodology is now compiled in this book. I am on a mission to get this process into the hands of as many people as possible—from teens to seniors and all seekers in between. Online, offline, in workshops, circles, at kitchen tables, in classrooms, boardrooms, coffee shops, and over a glass of wine—my goal is to share.

My hope is that the Life Blueprint process helps YOU. That you work through it step-by-step and author a plan for your life. That you are inspired to live fully beyond your wildest dreams and ride the waves of change, challenge, and sheer joy. This process, this book, my mission to share, is my wholehearted attempt to provide a method that helps everyone I reach to get very clear on who they are, what they stand for, what they want out of life, and how to make it happen. I wish that for every single person.

Enjoy and good luck!

Nicole

Within the Life Blueprint process there are various exercises. I have provided a QR code (flip to page 192) that will give you free access to the full-size printable worksheets and charts.

Introduction

The events that led to writing this book— a.k.a. why I wrote this book

My mom said I was reading at the age of two. Books abounded in my childhood home, and they abound in my home today. If there is a vacant space, I fill it with a book. There are bookcases and stacks of books everywhere—even in the bathroom and laundry room. And I even have some boxed up in storage—this actually causes me physical pain. I feel as though having these books in storage is a travesty. I miss their look and smell. Their multicolored spines and varying heights and textures . . . I could go on and on. But of course more than anything, I appreciate—no, I cherish—their contents. That a person poured their heart into sharing a story, a piece of themselves, touches my heart immeasurably. The way that art collectors treasure their collections and the work of many greats, I treasure the stories and learnings shared in books. I own more books than I will ever read cover to cover, and I continue to buy more without apprehension or remorse. I select them lovingly, carry them to the checkout, and take them home as though they are precious, fragile, easily bruised delicacies. Books are my outlet, my snack, my inspiration. As a child, I escaped into their imaginary worlds where there was peace, solitude, beauty, hope, and safety. The words *hope* and *safety* may seem new to you as they relate to the transcendent place that books take us; but for me, they are the most critical. My childhood was not smooth sailing, so into books I dove for refuge. It is not surprising that with the likes of

5

fairy tales and Dr. Seuss and fables around me as a child, then Judy Blume as an adolescent (the storylines and characters in her books were often based on people that came into her family's life), and autobiographies, biographies, and self-help books as an adult that I would lean into books to create my ideal life and also turn to them in times of need. The path that led to the development of the Life Blueprint process was due to a series of unfortunate life challenges. Though I aspired to live a "fairy-tale" life I certainly knew I would encounter witches and warlords (a.k.a. challenges) along the way. And I have certainly had my fair share of those encounters. In the end, I have prevailed, as I will share in the book. My fairy-tale ideals have certainly calmed. What has allowed me to not only survive but also thrive through life's many tailspins, witches, and warlords is the Life Blueprint process.

I have been on both sides of the proverbial coin. I have had some gut-wrenching losses and challenges and equally, some chaos-inducing wins. Both ends of the spectrum can turn our lives upside down.

I relentlessly searched for a guiding hand. In the process I did find resources, but they fell short. The solutions offered gave me pieces of the puzzle, but there was nothing that put it all together.

The challenges to which I refer have been deeply personal: marital breakdown, health issues, and a myriad of unexpected traumas. In all cases, their impact was overwhelming and threatened my very existence. To survive, I leaned into my strengths and successes in other areas of my life for guidance and hope. Though my personal life was a mess during these times, my work life remained consistent and on track. It's not that my work was free of challenges—it was not—but there was a disciplined acumen within me that allowed me to always make work, work. I was good at it. So, I leaned into what made me good at work—my decisiveness, my empathy, my strategic prowess, my creativity, and my relentless work ethic—and I tried to figure out how I could harness these traits and the processes I relied on in times of challenge and apply them to my personal life.

In business, there are standard business practices and protocols that we lean into for work that are relatively ubiquitous and universal. We accept these practices as vital to creating sustainable economic entities. The practicality of these systems and methodology is what has made them so widely and routinely accepted regardless of race, gender, or creed. However, no such broad sweeping systems or methodologies exist for human life. For every race, gender, culture, and belief system, there are often unique, varied, and disconnected practices. When my marriage crumbled, I crumbled, but I could not stay that way. I had to get "life" on track because I had a life and business to run. From a business perspective, the agency I had cofounded was now a multimillion-dollar operation with seventy employees, fifty-plus clients, and 5,000 brand ambassadors across the country. Growing the agency was no easy task. I had worked very hard to create an amazing team and make the company successful—our reputation was stellar, and our business was award winning. As I said, crumbling was not an option. My confidence professionally was high. My confidence personally was low, and so I took strength and learnings from work in order to rebuild my life.

I had a proven track record that started when I was a junior and quickly accelerated in brand management at Nestlé before being asked to manage a joint venture between Nestlé and Coke. From there, I was asked to lead a "new agency model" start-up for a holding company. The agency grew from zero to break even in less than eight months, multimillion in three years, and then on to eight figures and one of the strongest agencies of its kind in Canada. I was simultaneously building a new agency with the Andretti race team and creating unique profit center models in my own agency. I was in my element in the professional world and believed there had to be resources that I could apply to get my personal world back on track.

I leaned first and foremost into my strategic acumen. Strategists by nature are curious, avid explorers who love white paper reports, research, methodologies, and tools. In addition, they are often critical thinkers with an uncanny ability to clear through the clutter. I was determined to apply this skill to my situation. I think quickly and intuitively. I can see an idea from concept to completion, its strategic merit and executional requirements in minutes—much to the frustration of those in my circle, my children, colleagues, and even clients at times. In an attempt to regain the success and vision I had before my "happily ever after" collapsed, I evaluated everything that made me successful at work and leaned into that—heavily. I became a workaholic and figure-it-out-aholic. (I am also known for creating my own words.) It was in this spirit that I reengineered the strategic process that we use for business for our personal lives.

And it worked!

Today I am living a happily and fulfilled "ever after." Sure, I still face traumas and challenges, but I also have joy and lots of positive experiences and opportunities. Interestingly, sometimes even the good things in life can throw us off track, proving once again that we need a process.

ENTER LIFE BLUEPRINT

Life Blueprint is a fusion of the strategic processes (i.e., long-term and annual planning processes) we so easily, consciously, and with great discipline apply to work blended with the best in self-help motivation, transformation, mission/purpose clarity and goal-setting courses, books, workshops, and coaching.

The process allows you to create a plan that can evolve as you live, work, grow, and even change your mind. In addition, it provides you with gut-check parameters so if you do want to change your mind, you are doing so with very deliberate and conscious intent. It adds clarity and direction to the blur caused by fear and shock and puts a stake in the ground as to where you are at this moment, allowing you to intentionally evaluate the decisions you want to make and the paths you want to take moving forward.

Often as we unravel, we start to rebuild quickly and often without taking the time to think through everything because we are doing so from a place of fear and shock versus conscious intent. In the case of my marriage, and in the case of the agencies I co-built, I departed when the fundamentals were no longer working. To stay would have caused more harm than good. In both cases when I left, there were implosions and explosions—none of which I expected and which if I could turn back time, I would reconfigure to pave a better path toward mutual success for all parties. But this is hindsight. And at the time I did not have "the blueprint!"

My initial intent with the Life Blueprint process was to create a methodology to lean into when things crash and burn, when there are challenges or a fork in the road. It provides a way for us to reflect, realign, and poise ourselves for success before hastily picking a path, making a decision, or moving forward. It helps us find calm and figure out our next steps in the chaos and turmoil.

I created the process due to pain and loss and challenge. But I have also leaned into it in moments of success and joy. In my agency life, we became the Agency of Record for a Client—a win we pegged at one million dollars. Within months, it grew into a $6.5 million win, and while awesome, it nearly killed us as we worked all-nighters and unexpectedly built a team (a stellar team, I might add!). These moments of triumph can equally cause a degree of upheaval and even chaos and panic. Because Life Blueprint is a holistic approach, taking into consideration the breadth and depth of a multitude of aspects of our life, when things happen, it is a guidepost from which we can consciously iterate, pivot, or start over.

The process has helped me to survive several storms and achieve my goals. It is a living, breathing resource in my life. And that is why I called it a blueprint—it is a set of multilayered, multifaceted plans, each with their own context that when added together create a fabulous multidimensional life.

Borrowing from the world of architecture and design, blueprints allow us to create incredible structures with awareness of the land on which they stand, with firm foundations that allow them to weather storms, with rooms and spaces that have their own purpose and/or context, with walls and doors that create boundaries and/or privacy, with windows to let light in, and with a roof that points skyward to the heavens. We then design and redesign the inner and outer spaces as our life, our needs, and our tastes evolve. Apply this as an analogy to the Life Blueprint—it provides a process to help you consider the multitude of elements that matter in your life and how to holistically bring them together. It combines all that a person is and wants at a point in time. It then allows for a full plan to be created.

Most importantly, it puts a stake in the ground. It forces decisions to be made, and from there, we can move forward. We can course correct. We can adjust. We can move with awareness and intent. This is fundamental, for when we choose a course of action, identify where we are going, and outline the steps to get there, we make more conscious choices—and we end up getting to where we want to go. We achieve goals! Sure, there may be some twists and turns, but we will arrive at the destination at some point because we had a navigation plan.

The Life Blueprint gives much needed awareness and perspective that leads to understanding that leads to clarity. Clarity leads to focus. Focus leads to mastery. And with mastery, we have direction that fosters discipline and commitment, keeping us on track and inspired to live the life of our dreams!

SELF-ACTUALIZATION
Desire to become the most that one can be

ESTEEM
Respect, self-esteem, status, recognition,
strength, freedom

LOVE AND BELONGING
Friendship, intimacy, family, sense of connection

SAFETY NEEDS
Personal security, employment, resources,
health, property

PHYSIOLOGICAL NEEDS
Air, water, food, shelter, sleep, clothing, reproduction

Living fully in the direction
of your dreams

Discipline & commitment

Mastery

Clarity

Understanding

Awareness &
perspective

The Life Blueprint trajectory is akin to Maslow's hierarchy—a model we often refer to when doing strategic planning in the workplace. Abraham Maslow was an American psychologist who created a groundbreaking hierarchy of needs in his 1943 paper "A Theory of Human Motivation," in the journal *Psychological Review*. In Maslow's hierarchy, we rise from sustenance to self-actualization. With the Life Blueprint model, we rise from awareness and perspective to living fully.

The Life Blueprint model takes us through a variety of exercises that stimulate learning and awareness. When each element from the model is completed with respect to the other elements, a holistic, integrated plan results. We expect this when doing strategic planning for work. But a model for human life has escaped us until now.

I first launched the Life Blueprint process while doing some work as a part-time professor. I was teaching students business strategy and creative strategy and coaching a post-grad group of entrepreneurs. What I found was that what these students really wanted was life counsel. As soon as we got to Q&As or meetups, they asked very personal questions. At the time, some of my legacy agency clients also asked me to expand our offerings and run workshops and coach their teams. No longer was I being asked to create promotional materials but rather consult on health and wellness. Simultaneously, I also had friends leaning on me for support as they navigated divorces, aging parents, empty nesting, and middle-age malaise. And my own children were now transitioning into adulthood and the conversations were "big."

I started to share the methodology that I used to navigate work, life, relationships, goals, mission/purpose—the whole shebang! To be very clear, I am not a guru or a trained practitioner. I am a student of life. And if I learn something that I think is going to make someone else's life easier, then I share.

The more I shared the Life Blueprint process, the more the word started to spread. Today, I am on a continuous mission to expand access. It is available both online as a DIY digital course (with me leading each section over video) and offline as I speak, run workshops, and coach globally. This book is the intended "hard copy" of the methodology filled with how-tos and examples. My goal is to get it in the hands of as many interested continuous evolvers as possible—so please share!

There are successful examples in the book and testimonials on my website; however, I am the first and consistent test case and proof the methodology works. Today as I type, I am doing work that I love, and I wake up nine mornings out of ten eager to head into the day. Come on, no one's life is perfect. But life can be pretty damn great! In fact, it can be extraordinary if we create a plan. I have not settled for less and I hope you don't either—so let's get to it!

Extraordinary awaits!

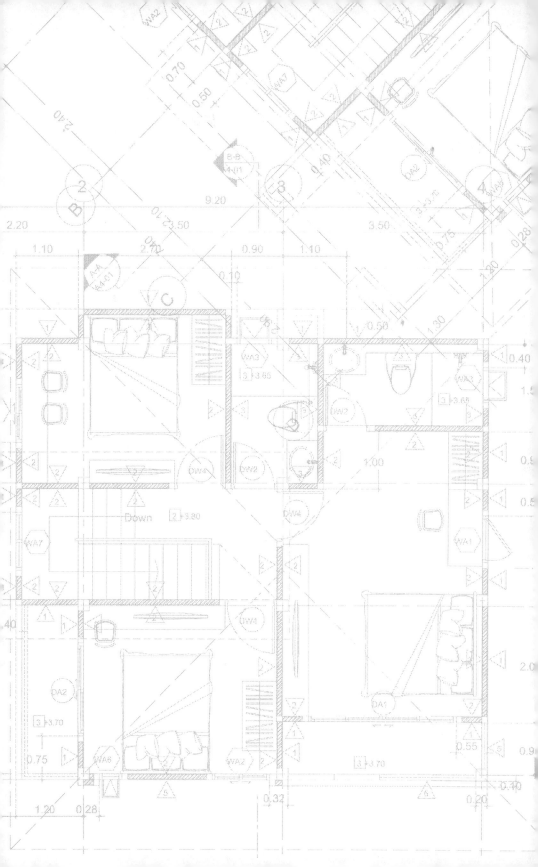

Questions you may have as you begin to create your extraordinary life

WHO IS THE PROCESS BEST SUITED FOR?

You! Admittedly and as objectively as appropriate, I think everyone will find the Life Blueprint process useful. Thousands of people have leveraged the process, and more are leveraging it every single day.

Ask yourself any one of these questions—and if you respond *yes* to even one, then the Life Blueprint process can help you:

1. Have you finished your education and are still unsure of what you want to do? *BAH Geography B ED French, geo EE*

2. Have you been in your career for a few years, but you are unsure if this is the career/profession that you want to pursue for the rest of your life?

3. Are you at a stage where you have everything that you were working toward, yet you feel unsatisfied?

4. Are you trying to balance work and life?

5. Are you trying to balance the long-term vision that you have for your life with living in the moment?

6. Are you tired of creating a list of goals, then being distracted for a million reasons and therefore not achieving them?

7. Have you put some dreams/goals to the side while taking care of/raising loved ones and now you want to make them happen?

8. Are you happy and have an idea that is niggling away at you that you want to explore but are afraid it will cause upheaval, or you don't know how or where to start?

9. Are you unsure of your mission/purpose?

10. Are you overwhelmed?

Yes, the Life Blueprint process will help you! I guarantee it works. Anyone who has committed to the process will tell you that it has provided clarity, direction, and focus, and that they achieved their goals sooner. And the beauty of the process is that it is not a one-and-done. It evolves with you as you evolve through life.

IS WORKING THROUGH THE PROCESS THE BEST USE OF MY TIME?

"Hell, yes!" is my answer, of course, but let me explain. The process is not a one-and-done.

Just as planning in business is a continuous process, so, too, is creating and then managing an extraordinary life. The Life Blueprint process requires you to do "the work." Once you go through the process from start to finish, you will iterate and update it for the rest of your life. It truly is a guide for life.

How much time you spend is really up to you. My advice: spend the time—it's your life.

And the value of your life—priceless!

Blueprint

Blueprint

HOW DO I RECOMMEND THAT YOU WORK THROUGH THE PROCESS?

Follow the process in order (there is a method to my madness!) and take it step-by-step. Some steps are quick, while others require time to ponder and then execute. And in some cases, you'll want to get creative and spend extra time.

Regardless of how you decide to allocate the time, be sure to do the checks along the way for consistency. This is why I prefer if people focus and do it all at once, within the span of a few days. When you start to extend it over long periods, you lose track and often have to go back and rework and rethink things.

I think the ideal/perfect world scenario is to do it over a weekend in a space where you can be on your own to ponder and manage time at your own pace. There is no right way or wrong way or exact time. Whatever you decide, I can confirm that the impact will be game changing! When we have a plan with a clear path, we move forward with ease and confidence. It is the greatest feeling!

WHAT DO I NEED?

All you *really* need is a pen and paper! I'm sharing the list below because these are the tools that I make available when I run Life Blueprint workshops. During the workshops, we create vision boards, draw, meditate, and even burn some shit! I make it interesting!

My intent in sharing the following details is to set you up for optimal success and to invite you to make the process fun for yourself. Life is a wild and extraordinary ride. Embrace the Life Blueprint process with an energetic, blissful mindset—this will poise you to do some great thinking while enjoying it!

Block the time

1. Time—allocate the time in your calendar. Mark off the hours or mark off the weekend retreat (even if it is a staycation). Literally book in the time as though it is a critical meeting that you cannot miss—because it is! It's a meeting with yourself to plan your life!

2. Healthy food, water, tea, coffee. You are going to do some hard but VERY worthwhile work, so set yourself up for success. I typically fill my fridge with healthy, easy-to-grab, feel-good foods. Having this easy access allows me to take needed breaks that fuel me for "the work."

3. A safe space—you will work through a lot of things throughout the process. It needs to be a judgment-free zone. You need to be able to close a door, silence disturbances around you, and focus. I often go away or head to my cottage for a solo weekend when I do this work. Solitude is key to doing "the work."

4. This book and the worksheets within it—we have tried to create the worksheets so you can either do them in the book, rip them out, or access them with the QR code provided throughout and at the end of the book and print them out. Whatever method you choose, I want you to be able to put some of them physically in front of you simultaneously— either on a desk or tabletop or taped to the wall (my option of choice). In order for each of the sections to be integrated and feel holistically connected, you sometimes need to see them all at once. You can also draw them out—they are not complicated.

5. Tape—that's because of the chosen option to tape key work to the wall. I do this, and once again, I guarantee it works! It will be explained when you get to that step.

6. Optional—laptop and printer—in case you want to print off the charts.

7. Optional—assortment of magazines on a myriad of different topics and interests, pictures, glue sticks, poster boards (two or three), scissors. You will be creating an assortment of vision boards. It is your call whether you create these physically (on a poster board) or virtually (on a PowerPoint slide, Pinterest board, or something equivalent). My recommendation is that you create real live boards.

vision boards

8. A journal—I like lined journals, but it's your preference. Writing for me is how I figure things out and do "the work." It has been proven by many, many people that when we journal, we clear our minds and sort through issues. I firmly believe we all should have been taught how to journal as we became

adolescents. Remember when we once had diaries? Why did we ever lose or not evolve that practice?

9. Music—it soothes the soul as you do the work. It has also been proven that country music and classical music are the best for our peace of mind and health. If they don't strike your fancy, I suggest that you pick happy music that plays ambiently in the background while you work.

True

10. You—you fully and completely. This is your life. Invest the time. If work required you to dedicate twenty-four hours to a project, you would do so without even thinking about it—because it's your job. Well, this is your life. Nothing—and I do mean absolutely nothing—matters more than your life! Spend the time. Do "the work." I guarantee it will be worth every single minute.

HOW DOES IT WORK?

The Life Blueprint methodology is a step-by-step process. Through-out I use examples and analogies to explain the importance of each individual step and its connection to the other steps. This is why it is a holistic, integrated process. Everything is given separate due diligence and then threaded together. Ultimately, this is why the process works. The two analogies I leverage the most are that of building a house and assembling a puzzle.

Leaning into the house analogy—you don't decide to build a house and it appears before you magically the next day. There are a series of steps required to build the house. And for the house to stand tall and strong and capture the intended vision that you have for it, it must be built step-by-step. Hence, the Life Blueprint step-by-step guide for creating an extraordinary life.

Ditto the puzzle analogy—you buy a box with the beautiful visual of the assembled puzzle on the exterior and hundreds of pieces that need to come together inside. In order for the puzzle to be complete, all the pieces must fit. Throughout the process, I will suggest that you take a break and go for a walk. Similar to when you are sorting through the box of a thousand puzzle pieces and you just can't seem to find the right one; or you find one, but it isn't the right fit. This will also happen with the process. You may have moments where the pieces don't seem to be fitting as comfortably as you would like, so you take a break and then return to sort through the box and find the right piece. Apply this thinking when you are working through the process and things don't feel right. Go for a walk so you can reflect and ponder what you have completed and what is and is not working. Return to the work you have completed for reference and then move forward. Working through the entire process step-by-step with the objective of a holistic actionable plan as the outcome will be achieved. I guarantee it!

There are ten steps. The order of the steps is intentional.

Skipping steps will result in a less than complete plan that may not be holistic or integrated. I cannot stress enough how important it is to go through the process step-by-step. One step leads to the next. Each step has its own context and reason for being, and I will do my best to explain, provide examples, and then connect the dots as you go through the process. Please trust that there is a "method to my madness."

The outcomes are unique to every single person because we are unique beings.

Most importantly, as you go through the process once, the process will serve you for the rest of your life. This is a critical point because by virtue of being a process, it consists of a multitude of variables and considerations, it is contextual (awareness of the impact of the past and the importance of the present and the future), and it is flexible. If things change, if you change, if you have a significant life event, you can go back to the process and reevaluate to see if everything still makes sense—if everything still fits together like perfectly connected pieces of a puzzle.

And last, I believe that we need to "begin with the end in mind." Leaning into the house and puzzle analogies, we have a vision as to what the final house we want to build will look like, and for the puzzle to work it needs to look like the picture on the cover. Applying these analogies to the Life Blueprint process, before you dive in, please read the following overview of the steps. The review will give you a sense as to what you will be working through and what the end result will be. While at this point, the work in each step is unknown and is yet to be done, having a sense of the different steps will help to guide you as you go through the process.

OVERVIEW OF THE LIFE BLUEPRINT STEP-BY-STEP PROCESS, SO YOU KNOW WHAT'S AHEAD AND HOW IT ALL COMES TOGETHER.

Vision = Dream BIG!

Groundwork—Analysis & learning before moving forward

Impact—Your unique story & impact/legacy

Values—The fundamental foundation

Mission—Daily reason for being

Goals—Get clear, prioritize

Game Plan—Actionable plans

Gut Check—Holistic, integrated alignment

Managing—Continuous evolution, iteration, or pivot

Live your BEST life!

Step 1. Dream Big—What is it you really want?

We dream daily about how life "could be." But what if you could make these dreams a reality? You can! In this exercise, we will set your mind free to dream big and unleash your goals and desires.

Step 2. Laying the Groundwork—Backward before forward

Like building a house, you will start to design the space in which you live out your best life by taking a "lay of the land." You will complete a series of exercises that will clear some mindset clutter (a.k.a. "baggage") and allow you to take stock of where you are right now. You will leave behind (or park) what no longer serves you, then move forward positively.

26

Step 3. What's Your Story—Begin with the end in mind

With your vision now set as your inspiration to keep moving forward, we will have a rather intense conversation on your legacy—the impact you "want" to have on others and the world. This exercise will focus not on "breaths you take" but on "the breaths you take away."

Step 4. Define Your Values—The foundation upon which everything rests

We tend to underestimate or take for granted the role that our values play in our lives. They are the navigation system, our GPS, the foundation for every decision we make, whether we consciously know it or not. Value-clarity is fundamental and in this step, you will get very clear in order to build a strong foundation upon which to build out the rest of your life plan. Just as the foundation for a home forms the base upon which the entire structure rests.

Step 5. Clarify Your Mission/Purpose—Resolve your reason for being

Note that this is Step 5. I am calling that out because so often people want to start here. While it is true that understanding our mission and purpose is vital to our daily existence, to ensure we are clear and define it based on our work and not on the opinions of others or life's pretenses, we must do the preceding steps first. As I said earlier, the order of the steps is intentional. Trust my process.

Step 6. Set Measurable/Tangible Goals—Get clear on what you want to achieve

With your vision as your "North Star," your legacy/impact as your "end," your values as your GPS, and your mission/purpose identified for this moment in time, you now have all the tools to list your goals. Rest assured, we will do some work on your goals, not only prioritizing them, but also giving them clarity, breadth, and depth.

Step 7. Create a Game Plan—Plot a plan and connect all the dots

At this point, we have done some amazing work. In this step, we start to bring it all together into an actionable plan that we can see, easily articulate, and therefore live and breathe every day. It really will become that easy. And as a result, your dreams will become your reality.

Step 8. Gut Check—Holistic alignment of the Total Blueprint for your life

This step was one of the fundamental reasons I created the process. You see, I had all the pieces from all my business planning practices, self-help books, coaches, mentors, and workshops, but I had done them all separately. Prior to me creating this fusion and all-encompassing process for our lives, there was nothing on the market that was cohesive, consistent, and integrated. A holistic plan is CRITICAL, and in this step, that will be the focus.

Step 9. Shit Will Happen—Continuous evolution, iteration, or pivot

Let's be honest, there are going to be some unexpected surprises and twists and turns in your journey. Add to this that you are going to achieve some of your goals, realize new opportunities, and seek new adventures. Here is the GREAT NEWS—this process is now embedded in your DNA. It's literally in you. As such, it is a tool that will become second nature that you can use in perpetuity.

Step 10. Live Your Best Life—It's yours in the making!

In this step, we will discuss how to keep the process alive and continuously move in the direction of your goals and dreams every day.

And then you are done!

It's easy.

It's hard.

Some steps are quick.

Some steps take time.

Some steps you will finish and then go back and adjust as you ponder or work through the next step.

My ask is that you make the commitment and go through the process. You would do this if it was part of your job.

THIS IS YOUR LIFE.

IT MATTERS.

YOU MATTER.

Only you can make this decision. Only you can make the commitment. I am here to guide, support, coach, and send virtual love and hugs. It is my mission to get this methodology in as many hands as possible. I truly believe it is critical to living fully, and I wish that for everyone.

Step 1

Dream Big—What is it you really want?

It is never too late to be who you might have been.

–George Eliot

Twenty years from now you will be more
disappointed by the things you didn't do than
by the ones you did do. So throw off the bowlines!
Sail away from safe harbor. Catch the trade winds
in your sails. Explore. Dream. Discover!

–Mark Twain

Tragedy is the difference between
what is and what could have been.

–Abba Eban

I am opening with the juxtaposition of these three quotes. Read them again, out loud, and absorb their individual meaning. I am attracted to quotes because they make me think. My intent with these three is to get you to think . . . differently. To think about the hopes and dreams you had or have.

As children when left to our own devices, we play, we pretend, we dream, we live very much in the present without much concern for the future. As children, very little if anything is expected of us—how nice! As we grow, discipline, rigor, and/or structure are added to our days. Perhaps some of this is for the better, and perhaps some not. And as we continue to age, the rigor, structure, and expectations increase.

Imagine if we went back to that curious, ever-present child within us and dreamed about the life we could have. Dreamed with abandon. Dreamed without the confines of discipline, rigor, and structure.

At this point, you may be wondering where I'm taking you. Full transparency—I am going to ask you to do a visioning exercise with me. The rationale is that I have likely walked in shoes similar to yours.

I graduated from university, got married, and got a great job in a successful company. I quickly rose through the organization and was given the opportunity to manage a joint venture between Nestlé and Coke. Then I was poached to do a start-up, a new agency model for a large agency holding company, which I did for a decade, growing it with my amazing team to rank in the top five agencies in the country. I then went on to do this for another agency before leaving to create a boutique agency that allowed me and my colleagues to do work we love while also evolving our personal passions. Hence the reason I have pursued my passion—teaching and evolving this methodology. It has become my mission. My reason for being.

I share this right now because I am asking you to trust me, to dream, to venture into the land of woo-woo. That can feel uncomfortable for many—especially those in the corporate world or those who struggle with the vulnerability of this intimate "work." I want you to know that I get it. So while you may be asking, "Really? Can we not just get on with it? Do I really have to do this?"

The answer is: "Yes! You really have to do it."

Creating a vision for your life is about getting clarity on what you want to achieve in the future. Having a clear vision can help you set meaningful goals and take the necessary action to turn your dreams into reality.

teaching @ pschool.

There are three key benefits to having a vision:

1. Direction—A clear vision can help you make better decisions, avoid distractions, and focus on what matters most. It can also give you a sense of purpose and direction.

2. Motivation—When you have a compelling vision, you are more likely to be motivated and inspired to take action and overcome obstacles. Your vision can give you the energy and drive to pursue your goals with passion and enthusiasm.

3. Resilience—A vision can also help you build resilience and cope with challenges and setbacks. When you have a clear sense of why you are doing what you do, you are more likely to stay committed and persistent in the face of adversity.

My ask as we begin this first step is that you dive in with reckless abandon. **Let go of the life you were supposed to have and create the life you want to have.**

I have felt your discomfort, and I am going to ask you to put it aside. Dreaming big is critical, and to do that, we need to free our minds. The dream vision you have inside you matters. **Investing**

the time to boldly imagine your best life is the worthiest investment of time you will ever make. I know that is a very bold statement. I believe it because I am proof that it works as are the many others who have worked through the Life Blueprint process. You likely invest time in people, in your jobs, in so many things. This is your life—invest in it for yourself. The dividends will be EXTRAORDINARY!

Have I made my case strongly enough yet? I hope so!

We are going to dream—not little dreams—**REALLY BIG DREAMS**. My goal here is to unlock your deepest desires. We will work through dreaming in two parts. First, you will do a creative visualization, then you will create a vision board. Once you complete the visualization, you are ideally going to bring it to life in a vision so you can see it, touch it, feel it, taste it. This is how it will become a reality.

To do the visualization, find a quiet place where you will not be disturbed for approximately thirty minutes. Have with you a blue pen and some paper and/or a journal. (Why a blue pen? Here is some woo-woo for you—blue is the color that represents the throat chakra. Ideally, this chakra helps us speak our truth. And when we lean into the color blue, which also represents the water and the sky, we have an enhanced sense of peace and mental clarity.) Once settled, put on your headphones/ear pods, and prepare to play some gentle acoustic music. Ensure you are comfortable. Follow my directions.

We are going to start by changing your physiology and your mood/mindset. To do this, I am going to ask you to take a series of four box breaths. Box breaths reconfigure your energy and physiology, bringing you into the present.

Once you complete the breaths, please turn on gentle acoustic music and read on.

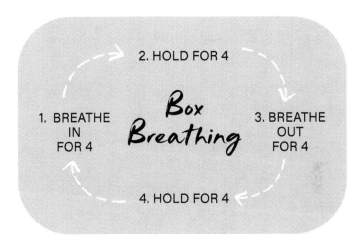

Breathe in for 4.
Hold for 4.
Breathe out for 4.
Hold for 4.

Breathe in for 4.
Hold for 4.
Breathe out for 4.
Hold for 4.

Breathe in for 4.
Hold for 4.
Breathe out for 4.
Hold for 4.

Breathe in for 4.
Hold for 4.
Breathe out for 4.
Hold for 4.

With the breaths complete, you are ideally in a relaxed state. Feeling peaceful with the soft meditative music playing in the background, follow the guided meditation below, and let yourself drift into a state where you dream.

Imagine yourself in a peaceful state.

You are sitting relaxed and looking out to the horizon.

Breathe in.

Breathe out.

Release all tension and just imagine . . .

Breathe in.

Breathe out.

Set yourself free.

Breathe in.

Breathe out.

Feel the complete freedom.

Imagine . . .

It's a beautiful day, and it's your favorite time of year—you love this temperature.

You are completely comfortable and at ease.

You can hear the birds and feel the gentle breeze flow through your hair and kiss your face.

The air smells fresh and reminds you of when you were a child and you would run with abandon.

Lean into that feeling of peaceful abandon.

Feel the peace and breathe easily.

Everything you want and need exists.

You are safe and sound.

You are happy, healthy, full of joy.

Imagine yourself feeling better than you have ever felt before.

Breathe in.

Breathe out.

You have arrived.

Your dreams are your reality.

It's all around you.

You can see them. Touch them. Taste them. Smell them.

Pause and keep breathing as these feelings build within you.

Feel all the good feelings.

Be unapologetic about how great you feel.

Breathe in.

Breathe out.

Now write it all down.

Capture all the feelings.

Capture all that you have created. Everything you have ever wanted has become a reality.

Write it down.

Let it spill on to the page.

Let the joy and all the feelings flow through your body, through your pen, and onto the paper.

Let it flow.

Imagine your arms spread out as you run in circles and laugh and fall to the ground and look up at the sky as you celebrate the achievement of everything you ever wanted.

Write down everything that you are feeling, thinking, seeing, smelling, touching, tasting.

Visualize your absolute greatest desires in every way.

Capture it all.

Capture where you are, what you see, who you are with, what you are doing.

Notice the surroundings.

Are you alone or are you with others?

What is your relationship to anyone who is with you?

Write until you have emptied out every thought and every feeling.

Write until you have nothing left to say.

Keep breathing.

Breathe in.

Breathe out.

Feel the sheer joy and peace and bliss as you write.

Let all this settle in.

Feel all the images that you see.

Imagine that you are in that reality.

Your dreams are your reality.

You are in them.

You can see everything, touch it, feel it, smell it.

Keep breathing.

Breathe in.

Breathe out.

Feel the love and peace all around you.

Feel the pride for what you have achieved.

See and feel these achievements.

Note their beauty and magnificence.

See yourself living in this dream.

Take in every detail and hold it all tight.

Keep writing.

Keep breathing.

Identify your greatest desires. Unleash them.

Embrace and accept every vision that you see and feel.

Go beyond your comfort zone.

Be limitless.

Believe that you are living everything you see, touch, taste, smell.

See yourself in the midst of all that you imagine . . . you are living the dream.

Visualize all that you desire . . . and more.

After you have finished capturing everything that you visualized, read it over.

Release the beauty of your visualizations to the Universe.

Let it support you in making your dreams come true.

Embody the energy and the feelings.

Take as much time as you need. Capture everything.

When you are done, read your visualization and relish in its magnificence. Feel all the feels.

The next part of the vision and dreaming process is to bring it tactically to life. To create a vision board that embodies your visualization. A vision board is a collection of images, quotes, and affirmations that represent your goals and aspirations. It's a powerful tool used to clarify and visualize your dreams, consistently reminding you to stay the course as you go along the path to making them a reality. For those who find creating a dimensional vision board a creative stretch, I am going to once again ask you to please give it a try. **If you want new or different answers or outcomes for your life, then you need to try new and different things!**

Remember earlier how I mentioned that you will require some or all of the following tools: printer, assortment of magazines on a multitude of different topics and interests, pictures, glue sticks, poster boards (two or three), scissors, and tape. Well, now you know why! Alternatively, you can grab images online and create an online board. The key is to choose a format that allows you to display your images in a way that inspires you.

In full transparency, I have included a picture of my current vision board. If you look closely, you will see it includes pictures of me in different areas. I am immersed in the board, just as I am immersed in my vision. And I would suggest you do the same.

Personally, I love creating a vision board. I do this annually, at a minimum. It typically takes me a few days to create a vision board.

I put the board and my clippings some-where where they cannot be disturbed and then over a period of days, I add pictures, quotes, and words to it, literally dropping them on the board as I collect them. Then one night when I am feeling peaceful, I will sort through them (usually while sipping a glass of wine with gentle music playing in the background) and begin to assemble them on the board. I keep some clippings, find more, remove others. If a picture feels as though it does not fit, I remove it.

My goal is to ensure everything feels as though it captures my vision for my future. I assemble the board and put everything in place, take one last look, then go to bed. In the morning, I review the board before gluing everything into place. Sometimes I make changes; sometimes I don't.

If creating a dimensional board still feels a little daunting, hopefully these simplified steps will help:

1. Gather inspiration—collect images, quotes, affirmations, a picture(s) of yourself to include . . . anything that represents your goals and dreams.

2. Choose a format—I really like using a reasonably sized piece of canvas/poster board (16x24). Other options include a bulletin board, a digital platform, or even PowerPoint.

3. Design your board—arrange your images on your board and use a glue stick or double-sided tape to secure them in place.

4. DISPLAY YOUR BOARD—yes, I wrote those words in all caps for a reason. You need to display your vision board where you will see it when you wake up in the morning, before you go to bed at night, and throughout the day. Mine is hanging on the wall that my bed faces so I easily see it when I am in bed. It's also the home screen for my laptop and phone. It is everywhere, so that I am continuously reminded to stay the course and to keep moving in the direction of my dreams!

Do vision boards really matter? YES!

I truly believe that **believing is seeing**! When we believe something, it becomes our reality—we know it must be so. When you are consistently seeing your vision board, it becomes your reality—you see it, and the visuals remind you of the vision you have for yourself, further ingraining this in your belief system.

The truth is, vision boards have been used for centuries.

with dad.
– paper & magazines.

The History of Vision Boards

ANCIENT TIMES
Ancient Egyptians used hieroglyphics to visualize their goals and aspirations.

20TH CENTURY
In the mid-20th century, psychotherapist Dr. Viktor Frankl used visualization techniques to help his patients overcome trauma and depression.

21ST CENTURY
Today, vision boards are a popular tool used by people around the world to manifest their dreams and create their ideal lives.

In the corporate world, we often allocate days to creating and then clarifying a vision and plan for our enterprises. We do this because it brings the team together to jointly align and commit to making it happen. And it works—witness all the HUGE companies that started off in garages (i.e., Amazon, Apple) or desks in a bedroom (Facebook/Meta) with founders who at the time were touted as "crazy" and who now lead some of the biggest enterprises in the world. Embrace your HUGE Dream. Your life is your enterprise!

Once you complete your vision board, you will see and feel the impact. Vision boards offer some very critical benefits:

1. Increased motivation—When you see your goals and dreams every day, right in front of you, you are motivated to keep moving forward. And you will see that by the end of the Life Blueprint process, you will have an action plan that accompanies the vision board. This adds to your motivation and inspiration because you can then see how you are contributing to it daily to bring it to life.

43

2. Improved clarity and focus—You will hear me say this more than once. **Clarity breeds focus and focus breeds motivation.** Creating a vision board requires you to identify your priorities and focus on what matters most to you. When things spiral, your vision board will help to navigate. You may make some adjustments, but you will know the direction you are headed.

3. Enhanced creativity—Designing a vision board allows you to unlock your creative side and explore new ideas and possibilities. Imagery makes it feel real, which is critical to achievement. When we can see it, feel it, and put ourselves in the context of the imagery created, we become consciously and unconsciously committed to making it happen. Anecdotally, in my live workshops, I consistently get feedback that people want more time to work on their vision boards.

Let me now give you some proof points that vision boards really do work.

A few years ago I ran a live Life Blueprint workshop. At the time I called it "A Day for a Decade." People attended the one-day workshop, and in the process, we created their plan for the next decade. Interestingly, I had four pairs in the workshop: two middle-aged couples, one couple under the age of thirty, and two business partners.

One of the pairs was a young couple who had been traveling and were working in my country for another year before moving to Europe. They were debating marriage, children, careers . . . pretty much everything.

They each created their own vision board, and at the end, they shared. Each of them had spent time really thinking about their careers, and one identified that they wanted a job change. Marriage and children were in the cards for both, though with slightly different timelines. And neither wanted to move back to their home country. Rather, they wanted to be in a neighboring country where they could be close to home but where they thought their lives and careers would be fuller. Fast-forward a few years and they are engaged, one in a new profession (an offshoot from their previous career), they are in a child-friendly home, and they have aligned on a timeline that feels good for both of them. They are a quick one-hour plane ride or four-hour train ride from their parents' homes and blocks away from a sibling. Their vision boards allowed them to have some interesting conversations and then work toward supporting each other in the achievement of their dreams.

Of the middle-aged couples, one ended up separating as they came to realize that blending their families and their life choices were not aligned. Their vision boards clearly reflected incongruent perspectives with alignment being something that they did not want to work toward. They respectfully set each other free. The second couple experienced the most dramatic shift. Their boards were independently codependent. Their boards embraced their full individual potential in complete harmony with the other person. From here, the two created an action plan, and today, they are living the life they cocreated that day. They left their high-powered influential corporate jobs, transitioned to digital nomad work, and are traveling the globe. They are happy, healthy, and very fulfilled.

The last pair were two business partners. While they were similar in age, they were at different life stages. One married late and had a child under the age of ten. The other was divorced with a son who had graduated university and was well into his career. Their goal in doing the workshop together was to independently figure out their long-term goals and then cocreate how they were going to work together and the impact on their company. At the end of the session, they realized they were in different but complementary places and could divide and conquer work differently than they had in the past. They had also put some pet projects on the back burner, and they realized that they needed to move these forward, as these projects would help them to reconnect better with each other. The workshop also provoked a lot of conversation about the health and well-being of their team. In an effort to move forward positively and sustainably, each team member was invited to attend a Life Blueprint workshop and then we ran a team workshop where we applied a version of the methodology for business to their company. The entire process was extremely motivating for everyone.

> When we are lost or in need of alignment—defer to the process. It helps to objectively create clarity.

Each team member had their own plan. And as a team, they had cocreated a plan for their company. Today, the team is still all together. Work is flowing in, and they have launched a new venture and are super excited about the future.

I do one last exercise to close off the Dream Big step, but let me provide some context first. I believe in rituals. Please indulge me for a moment as I share with you the importance of rituals, because this will not be the last time that I ask you to do one.

Rituals are symbolic actions, gestures, and words that are performed in a special and/or sacred way; sometimes, they can be an act that you do repetitively (or not). Rituals have been part of human culture since ancient times. They can take many forms, ranging from religious and spiritual rituals (such as prayer, meditations, or sacraments) to personal and daily rituals (such as morning routines, exercise, or bedtime rituals) and social ones (such as birthdays, weddings, holidays, or cultural celebrations). They can help people connect with the divine, express gratitude, or seek protection. Rituals can also help create and strengthen social bonds. Sharing a ritual with others can foster a sense of belonging, trust, and cooperation.

It has also been proven that rituals can have psychological benefits, from reducing stress and anxiety to increasing self-awareness and optimism. They mark something; and in the marking, we physiologically take note. And in taking note, we are reminded of the ritualistic act when we lose track, when we are triggered, when we fall off course, or when something great happens and we bear witness to the positive steps we have taken to make things happen. Which leads me to the first ritual I am going to ask you to do.

As it relates to Dreaming Big, my ritual is to share the sacredness of my dreams. I make a copy of my written visualization and my vision board. I fold them up, take them out to my garden, and I plant them in the soil. **Dreams are the seeds of a future reality. If we plant them and nurture them, they will grow.** We often hear the sentiment, "Where your energy flows, things grow," so I plant my "dream seeds," literally and figuratively. I plant them in my garden, ideally around flowers or in a place I love. In doing this, I will have shared my sacred dreams with the Universe and planted proverbial seeds. I invite you to do the same. For those who live in a flat or apartment or condo, plant them deep in a pot with a plant you love. This simple act will remind you of the importance of your dreams.

And if you think I'm a little too woo-woo or out there—let me ask you, what have you got to lose? Trust me, all these little tips and tricks will impact you and help support you daily as you create the life of your dreams.

Try it.
You just might
like it!

Having now dreamed your big dream and planted your "seeds," we need to create the plans that will support them and bring them to life. Leaning into my house blueprint analogy—when you design a home, you start with the end vision of what you want the house to look like. Having completed Step 1 of the Life Blueprint process, we now have a vision for what you would like your life to look and/or be like. This vision will now serve as inspiration and a guiding light as we develop the balance of our plans. To further connect the blueprint analogy and the Life Blueprint process together, I am going to use the structure of a house to explain.

Our vision is represented by the roof of the house, pointing skyward, inviting the balance of the structure to develop protected under its guiding protection.

VISION:				
Mission/Purpose:				
Goal:	Goal:	Goal:	Goal:	Goal:
Plans & timing to achieve each goal:				
Values:				
Key Factor for Success:				

You will start to see this visual now in several places throughout the book. I will explain each section as we go through the step-by-step process. With the completion of Step 1, we have established the look and feel of the house and all that it inspires. The rest will all make sense and fall into place as we work through the other steps. The next step in our construction process is to prepare the ground.

Before we move to the next step, I want to link the Life Blueprint to corporate strategic methodologies. If you recall, I explained at the beginning of the book that Life Blueprint is the reengineering of many of the processes we lean into consistently in the business world to ensure healthy, sustainable enterprises.

On an annual basis we conduct:

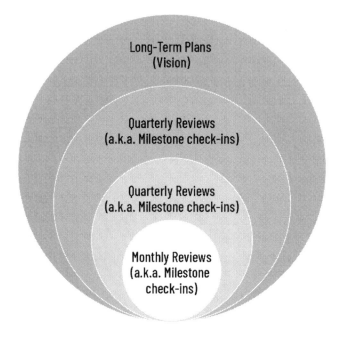

Long-term plans—Companies often gather key management from a broad spectrum of their teams to meet for a few days once a year to review the long-term vision for the company. The long-term vision usually spans a five-to-ten-year horizon. Often there are only slight updates and iterations to the plans. But there are times when there is a complete overhaul. Overhauls are due to significant achievements or challenges or changes in the business environment/world. The good news is that with a commitment to the process and with a history of planning, the decision to make changes is simplified because there is a structure in place.

- As it relates to Life Blueprint—in the first step you completed the vision exercise to determine the trajectory of your life. This is powerful. In future steps, I will provide direction on checking back on this vision annually, but for now you have put an important stake in the ground and claimed your future vision.

Annual business reviews—These review past and present performance against a multitude of metrics and are, as the name suggests, done annually. They often include analysis on the overall category/market, key competitors, regional and target analysis, and goals with action plans, to name just a few of the important and relatable items. These reviews drill down deep to uncover challenges and opportunities for the company. Obviously, these have a one-year horizon, but they lean into past performance, present performance versus plans, and the future, as far as one to three years out, with the key focus being on the twelve months ahead.

- As it relates to Life Blueprint—in Step 2, you will be doing some intense work that will uncover some things you need to be aware of, deal with, or choose to let go of from your past. This will be some soul-searching work. But it will set you up for success, and that is the key.

Quarterly and monthly reviews—These are smaller check-ins that also assess performance versus plan.

- As it relates to Life Blueprint—in the latter steps, I will ask you to identify key steps toward the achievement of your goals so you can track your own accountability and performance. In addition, I will ask you to note certain days/times in your calendar to check in on your goals and priorities. Think of these as milestone check-ins to ensure things are moving forward and any challenges/opportunities are being addressed and any adjustments made.

After completing each step, you will start to see their importance, their interconnectivity, and their resonance with the corporate strategic process. All of this is intended to provide context and the motivation to complete the entire Life Blueprint process and set yourself up for success.

Companies often also use the house visual and the concentric circles as tools to explain to their teams how everything comes together. My hope is that this also helps to further demonstrate to you the interconnectedness of the Life Blueprint process. I am convinced this is why it works. We literally work through every key aspect of life and bring it all together in one framework, then create action plans to make it happen!

Step 2

Laying the Groundwork— Backward before forward

"So, you want to build a house?"

To this day, I remember the contractor looking at me and asking this question. With drawings and pictures I had assembled on a board reflecting the beautiful images of the house my family and I wanted in one hand and my checkbook in the other, I was ready to go. We had the land, we had the plans, we had the money, we had mortgage approval from the bank, and we had ideas for all the materials. We had all the "things."

This, however, was not the contractor's "first rodeo." In less than five minutes, with a speech he had likely given many, many times, he proceeded to share that this was going to be a "process." My expectation to "start tomorrow" was lovely, albeit overzealous. We needed to do some groundwork before we could commence the build. While this totally made sense, I must admit I was a little deflated. I thought, couldn't we just dig the hole and start today?

Aah, no!

I share this story because with our visions and dreams identified, we often just want to jump right in and get started. While that is awesome, it often does not set us up for success. In fact, not taking the time to think things through, create a plan, and do "the work" can stunt, halt, and sometimes even shatter our dreams. Borrowing from the wisdom of my contractor, "We need to understand the lay of the land." In other words, we need to work through some details, we need to do a survey, we need to understand setbacks and holdbacks (in building terms, these are the issues that can impact design) and then we can finalize everything and pull it together into a cohesive plan. I knew this with the house. And I knew this about work. When clients approach us with issues or opportunities, or at work when we are faced with challenges, we always take a step back before we jump in. We have annual and long-term planning sessions, quarterly reviews, weekly status meetings. So many structures and processes keep us on track. We lean into these processes so that we set the business up for sustainable success. Why, oh why, do we not do this in our personal lives? Why don't so many of us take this time? Why don't we follow a structured process to achieve the life of our dreams? Why do we just state the intended outcome and expect everything to fall into place? Why?

I don't think we are ever actually taught to take the time to work through a process that sets us up for life success. I think we have been led to believe that doing so would be self-indulgent. I think we are often given a set of expectations by our parents with a path to achievement that they expect us to follow, and off we go. Or we decide, heck no, and follow our own path, but we rarely take the time to actually map it all out. I also don't think that an end-to-end complete process was ever provided. From someone who owns hundreds of self-help books, has taken the courses, and talked to the coaches and mentors, I can tell you that everyone offers a piece of the puzzle, but no one put it all together into a cohesive, integrated process . . . until now! So, let's get to it!

With our vision in front of us, let's do the dirty work! This truly is the "dirty work" step. We are going to look at the setbacks and holdbacks that play in our minds daily and often impede us entirely or slow down the process for moving forward and achieving our dreams. In this step, you will do some reflective work to gain awareness of patterns that may contribute to or hinder the achievement of your goals and dreams.

This step is divided into seven subsections. I will provide context for each, and you will work through the exercises in each section in sequence. And at the end, you will lay out your work so you can see it all together. Laying out all your work and reviewing it or taping it to the wall (hence, the tape in the list of tools) is something I will ask you to do frequently in the process for the purpose of review and rumination. I refer to this as doing a "gut check." It helps to ensure everything is consistent. While we dive deep and give each exercise the focus it needs and deserves, we often need to see how all the work starts to accumulate, note the collective learning, ensure integration, and then move forward to the next step.

And one last point. Some of this work is going to be soul-searching. My ask is that you stick to it—because trust me, it will be worth it—and very importantly, to withhold judgment. Please, please do not judge yourself throughout the entire Life Blueprint process. Judgment will not serve you. It will only hold you back, so please, let it go.

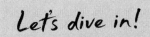

TAKING STOCK—PRESENT STATE

Picture a diver. We see them step up to the platform and dive into the water. But the truth is, before they dive in, they go into the water and get a feel for the surroundings. They ensure it is safe, and they plan their descent while in the water looking up at the platform. Once they can "see" themselves safely diving into the water, they get out, climb up to the platform, walk to the end, plan their dive, and dive in, knowing what is below them.

Right now, we are going to swim in the water. We are going to check things out before we dive into creating our future. As we do this deep-dive work, we are going to reflect on the learnings and decide what we are going to take with us and what we are going to leave behind because it no longer serves us.

We are going to start with an expansive exercise that helps you think about the various aspects of your life. I refer to this exercise as "Taking stock—present state." For those readers who are or have coaches, this may feel similar to a wheel of life exercise.

The intent of this exercise is to focus on what really matters to you. **When we focus, we achieve and our whole life is elevated.** Research shared by the National Library of Medicine showed that the **"Achievement of goals is positively related to life satisfaction."**

There are many aspects to life satisfaction, from work to relationships to money . . . you get it. Here's the thing: everything cannot be a top priority every day. You need to choose or get clear on your top priorities and decide how much focus you want to bring to them. Be honest with yourself and call it like it is.

Relative to the business strategic process, this part of the Life Blueprint process is akin to elements in the annual, quarterly, and monthly reviews where we determine priorities and then assess how we are doing against them given the current market situation.

As you do this, there is a "trick" of sorts that I want you to do as you complete this exercise: I want you to time yourself. Set a timer for three minutes. That's as much time as I want you to give yourself—just three minutes (or less). By doing the exercise with the least amount of thinking possible, and without judgment or second-guessing yourself, you will reveal what is *really* important to you—not what you may be tempted to think *should* be important.

Fill out the chart that follows by ranking the following priorities from 1 to 8, with 1 being a top priority and 8 your lowest priority. Then, in the second row, assess how you are doing right now with each of them by giving them an A, B, or C evaluation.

Parameter	Health	Partner/ Relation- ship	Family, Children, Parents, Siblings	Friends, Social Life	Job/ Career	Money	Religion/ Spirituality	Volunteer/ Impact/ Charitable Work
Priority 1-8 1= Top priority 8= Least priority								
Assess how you think you are doing A=All good B= Could be better C= Area for development								

Access full-size printable charts using the QR code on page 192

That was a fast three minutes!

Review your chart.

How do you think you are doing at present in terms of putting your time and energy toward your top priorities? Reflect for a couple of minutes, then put this exercise to the side, but hold on to it, because we are going to do it again later in the process. You can tape it to the wall with some of that tape (remember I mentioned using tape earlier?). As I work through the steps, I like taping key charts to the wall as I work through the process. It helps me to ensure consistency and connectedness. I will suggest this a few times throughout the process. (Don't get too excited yet, but I also have some exercises that upon completion, I advise you to burn the pages! Some charts/pages you will keep and paste on the wall; others you will burn!)

Next—and in an intentional order—we are going to work through six key factors that impact us in the achievement of our goals and dreams: fears, limiting beliefs, challenges, distractions and derailers, accomplishments, and strengths. Each of these areas has its own exercise for you to work through. In them, you will go beyond the esoteric and define the learning and greater effects on your life. With these exercises, you will note your feelings and begin to understand how what we feel impacts our life choices. This will ensure that everything "feels" right when we start to move forward.

I am an optimistic person, so for this section, we are going to first deal with some of the areas that might disrupt your success, and then we'll end on a high note. Let's start by talking about your fears, limiting beliefs, challenges, and distractions and derailers. These things clog your thoughts and your time, deplete your energy and inspiration, cause you to spiral and lose interest, and can seriously affect your health and well-being. But here's the thing: You give them this power! So, you can also take it away!

In the next few exercises, I have provided you with some charts to complete. Each chart has instructions on how to work through them followed by real-life examples of how I, or others who have attended my Life Blueprint workshops, have completed them.

FACTORS THAT IMPACT THE ACHIEVEMENT OF GOALS AND DREAMS

☐ Factor 1: Fear

Let's "start" with fear. I put the word *start* in quotes because often starting is in itself our greatest fear! Fears are often unknowns or experiences we do not want to have (or do not want to have again). And they can be paralyzing. However, with closer examination, we can look at the ones that are holding us back and limiting our potential. Then we can choose how we want to manage them so we can live fully and pursue our goals and dreams. We can put our fears in their place!

The power of fear: Understanding its impact on our lives

Fear is a universal emotion that affects us all. It can either hold us back or propel us forward. Fear is a basic emotion that is triggered by danger or threat. It is a natural reaction that prepares us for fight or flight. Essentially, fear is the body's protective response to perceived or actual harm. There is a wide range including phobias, social fear, and general anxiety disorder. Fear can either be debilitating or motivating, depending on how we respond to it. It can influence our physical, emotional, and mental well-being, affecting everything from our sleep to our performance at work.

Critical to managing our fears is to first understand fear itself. Though not a therapist, I have done a lot of reading on fear. I wake up panicked/anxious almost every morning with a list of fears running through my head. To cope, I have had to do the work to manage these and set myself up for success. What follows is a brief synopsis of some of the learnings that I have had in an effort to first understand, second identify, third note the impact, and fourth manage. And the irony of the situation is that just as I address a fear, I push myself to a new limit, often setting off a new round of fears—ugh!

Understanding Fear

Types of Fear	Fear of failure, fear of rejection, fear of the unknown	Gaining an awareness and understanding of fear in order to manage it and create a path for rational decision-making and action.
Sources of Fear	Past experiences, beliefs, cultural issues, trauma	Recognizing the stimuli for fears helps to increase understanding and manage/mitigate the impact.
Fight or Flight Response	A desire to run, hide, escape, or avoid a situation	An awareness of natural responses to a fear or something that triggers it can help to manage the response.
Desensitization	Facing fears gradually and consistently	With time and the building of confidence, fears can be reduced and sometimes terminated.

As we work to understand fear and how to manage it—it is interesting to note the types. While some fears are instinctual, some are learned, and some are rooted in the unknown.

The Science of Fear

Fear Type	Description
Instinctual	Immediate reaction to perceived threat.
Learned	Developed fear based on past experiences or cultural conditioning.
Existential	Fear of unknown or future events and outcomes.

Understanding the different types of fear helps us to recognize and manage them more effectively.

In understanding the types of fear, we also need to be aware that some are positive and some are negative.

Positive impact	Negative impact
Alerts us to danger. Fear is our body's natural warning system, alerting us to potential danger and helping us to avoid risky situations.	Physiological ailments (noted below)
Motivates us to take action. Fear can motivate us to take action and achieve our goals, encouraging us to step out of our comfort zone and try new things.	Interpersonal/relationship challenges, creating mistrust and preventing us from forming deep, lasting connections with others.
Bolsters creativity. Fear can stimulate creativity by forcing us to look for new ways to solve problems and adapt to changing circumstances.	Cognitive impairment, making it difficult to concentrate or remember information.

The physiological impact of fear:

Impact on physical state:

- Chronic fear and anxiety have been linked to a range of health problems, including heart disease, depression, and digestive issues.

- Increased heart rate, rapid breathing, sweating, and muscle tension are all physical responses to fear.

- The release of stress hormones, like adrenaline and cortisol, can impact the body negatively in the long term.

Impact on mental state:

- Triggers include past negative experiences, uncertainty, and fear of the unknown.

- Increased anxiety and the risk of depression.

- Negative self-talk and self-doubt, which can be harmful to our self-esteem.

- Procrastination, preventing us from taking action.

- Limited thinking, preventing us from seeing opportunities and possibilities.

I don't think it is a surprise to anyone that fear affects us greatly, so let's talk managing mechanisms.

Conquering Fear

Everyone experiences fear, but it is up to each of us to decide how we will react to it. Below are some strategies to help you overcome your fears:

Identify your fear	Recognizing and naming your fears can help minimize their impact.
Create a plan of action	Identify specific actions you can take to overcome your fear and increase your confidence.
Challenge negative thoughts	Challenge negative self-talk and replace it with positive affirmations.
Gradual exposure	Gradual exposure to your fear can help you feel more comfortable and confident.

As you can see, I have done a lot of work on understanding and managing fear! In the spirit of sharing is caring, I hope that some of what I have shared helps you.

With a better understanding of fear, let's start to do the work of naming and then managing your fears.

In the first column, list everything you are afraid of. In the next column, ask yourself how this fear may be holding you back. In the third column, try to think of some ways to overcome this fear and/or how you can manage it so it does not hold you back (the example chart may provide some useful prompts).

FEARS List everything you are afraid of—from spiders to starting a new business to finding a partner ...	IMPACT What impact is this fear having on your life?	PUTTING FEAR IN ITS PLACE What are the ways that you could manage/mitigrate/ eliminate this fear?

Access full-size printable charts using the QR code on page 192

Example:

FEARS List everything you are afraid of - from spiders to starting a new business to finding a partner ...	IMPACT What impact is this fear having on your life?	PUTTING FEAR IN ITS PLACE What are the ways that you could manage/mitigrate/eliminate this fear?
Flying	Stops me from traveling, especially with loved ones. Prevents me from exploring the world. Prevents me from visiting family in other places.	Consider taking a supplement that would relax me (Gravol makes me sleep—take it just before I get on the plane). Prep myself with movies, music, a book.
Failure	Stops me from even trying new things. I have ideas all the time but as soon as I share with my family, they shoot them down before I can even explain.	Actually try one of my ideas. Speak to someone positive—get a coach. Consider what the worst-case scenario is (in most cases it is not so bad).
Losing money/ financial ruin	I watch my money so closely that I don't even enjoy myself. I have money saved in the bank, in an RRSP and a TFSA. I pay all my bills and have minor debt. I am great at saving, but there are some things I could do to live more comfortably and maybe even go out for dinner, travel, go out with friends.	Create a financial plan that shows me that I will be able to live and save and have a healthy financial future.

Example strategy for overcoming a fear:

FEAR: PUBLIC SPEAKING ANXIETY

- Many people fear public speaking, which can limit career growth and social opportunities.

STRATEGY TO OVERCOME THE FEAR:

- Practice makes perfect. Start small by speaking in front of a supportive audience and gradually increase exposure.

OUTCOME DUE TO MANAGING THE FEAR:

- Growth and success.
- Overcoming this fear can lead to greater self-confidence, career advancement, and personal satisfaction.

Obviously there are fears that require support from a medical doctor and/or therapist. The goal of this exercise is to identify your fears and deal with the ones you can on your own. Get support for managing any of your fears where you need it. And then respectfully move forward in the direction of your goals and dreams without being held back by your fears. It doesn't mean you won't deal with them; it just means they will hopefully no longer prevent you from moving forward.

The benefit in understanding and confronting your fears is the gaining of awareness of their existence, their impact, and your determination to live fully. Rather than letting fear control us, we can learn to use it to our advantage. By reframing the fear and/or its hold on us, we can turn it into a valuable tool for growth and development.

You can use fear to push yourself out of your comfort zone and try new things. It can motivate you to work harder to achieve your goals and overcome the odds; and as a result, there will be growth and learning.

Bottom line, fear is a natural and important emotion. It is a living contradiction—keeping us safe on one hand and holding us back on the other. Awareness and understanding can help us manage and/or overcome it effectively. By taking small and deliberate steps to confront fear, we can experience growth, confidence, and personal satisfaction.

FACTORS THAT IMPACT THE ACHIEVEMENT OF GOALS AND DREAMS

☐ Factor 2: Limiting beliefs

Akin to fears, limiting beliefs prevent us from living our best lives. Different from fears, limiting beliefs are often the voices in our head that tell us *why* we can't do something. These voices tell us we aren't smart enough. We aren't capable. We don't have enough experience. The voices and their remarks keep us small. Sometimes these voices and remarks are our own. But most often, they are something someone else has said to us. The best way to squash these voices and these thoughts is to address them.

What Are Limiting Beliefs?

Limiting beliefs are negative thoughts or assumptions that we hold about ourselves, others, and the world around us. They often stem from our past experiences and can create barriers to personal growth and success.

Examples	Characteristics	Impact
I'm not enough. I don't have enough experience. I'll never be able to acheive that.	They are self-defeating, irrational, and often go unchallenged.	Limiting beliefs can hold us back from reaching our full potential and experiencing happiness.

With that understanding, there are several types of limiting beliefs:

- Core beliefs—deep-rooted beliefs about ourselves or the world around us that shape our thoughts and behaviors.

- Money beliefs—beliefs about our financial situation and what we believe to be true about money.

- Relationship beliefs—beliefs about ourselves and others that can impact our ability to form and maintain healthy relationships.

- Success beliefs—beliefs related to our skills, abilities, and potential for success.

And unfortunately, these limiting beliefs limit us:

- Emotionally—causing anxiety, stress, and low self-esteem, making it difficult to achieve our goals and enjoy life.

- Physically—causing symptoms like headaches, high blood pressure, and digestive issues.

- Socially—causing us to isolate ourselves and limit our social interactions.

The antidote → identification!

How to Identify & Overcome Limiting Beliefs

IDENTIFY THE BELIEF
Become aware of the negative beliefs that are holding you back.

CHALLENGE THE BELIEF
Ask yourself if the belief is really true or helpful.

REPLACE THE BELIEF
Choose a more positive and empowering belief to replace the old one.

Work through the chart by listing your limiting beliefs in the first column, their source in the second column, whether or not they are true in the next column, and how to get rid of/reframe them in the final column:

Limiting Belief	What is the source of this belief? Consider: Who said it? Where did it come from? What was the context?	This belief is not true. Identify the impact it is likely having on you.	Identify how you can get rid of this belief. What can you do so that you no longer even think about it?

Access full-size printable charts using the QR code on page 192

Example:

Limiting Belief	What is the source of this belief? Consider: *Who said it? Where did it come from? What was the context?*	This belief is not true. Identify the impact it is likely having on you.	Identify how you can get rid of this belief. What can you do so that you no longer even think about it?
I am not smart enough	When I was 13, I told my family I wanted to be an MD—they laughed and said that would never happen because I was not smart enough. My siblings laughed at me as my dad said this to me from across the room.	My family's response really hurt my feelings. And I believed them and thought they were right. I wasn't a great student, but I wasn't learning things that I was interested in.	I have done a lot of things that my family did not think I could do. Truth is I am smart enough and I need to believe in myself.
Other people have already had my idea	It's a fact. I have seen books that are very similar to the one I want to write. I don't think any of my thoughts or ideas are original.	This belief is stopping me from writing. I love writing, and I would love to write a book. It is actually making me sad.	I could actually start to write small posts and see what responses are like. Or I could just write for myself because it makes me happy!
I don't have enough money	I have always lived in a family where money is tight, so we never took any risks. I am worried that by chasing my dream, I won't have enough money and will suffer greatly.	This has made me hold back from trying so many things and pursuing my dream. I have always had enough and will always have enough.	I can put together a financial plan so that I can map out how much money I need to save so that I can make my goals happen and still be able to live.

The real benefits of overcoming limitations are that through awareness you realize they are not real. They are sabotaging misplaced beliefs that you can overcome if you so desire.

The Benefits of Overcoming Limitations

INCREASED PRODUCTIVITY
Better time-management and focus lead to getting more done in less time.

IMPROVED HEALTH
Reduced stress, fear, and anxiety can contribute to better mental, emotional, and physical health.

ENHANCED CREATIVITY
Breaking down beliefs and boundaries can result in new ideas, perspectives, and solutions.

GREATER PERSONAL GROWTH
Challenging oneself and learning new habits, skills, and attitudes contribute to personal and professional growth.

Bottom line, limiting beliefs can hold us back from being our best selves. By identifying and overcoming these beliefs, we can unlock our true potential and live a happier, more fulfilling life. Make the choice to let them go!

FACTORS THAT IMPACT THE ACHIEVEMENT OF GOALS AND DREAMS

☐ Factor 3: Challenges

Remember your last job interview when the interviewer asked you to name your "weaknesses" and/or "areas for development" and/or "challenges"? You likely cringed inside but were prepared; after all, everyone asks this question, so we all have an answer ready that is usually superficial but gets us through the interview and provides fodder for discussion. Well, this exercise is not that!

In this exercise, I want you to be honest with yourself and identify areas that are challenges for you and/or shadows. No superficiality here. The point here is not to beat ourselves up for what we are not, but through identification, find solutions for mitigating these issues so they don't negatively impact us or hold us back. This may mean getting support or coaching or finding tools or people to offset any issues.

Everyone faces challenges and weaknesses in life. But with the right strategies, we can learn to manage them and grow stronger.

And interestingly, the exercise that follows is about distractions and derailers. There is an interconnection here with challenges. I find that one of the biggest issues with this last factor is that it actually impedes us from dealing with our challenges! As if our challenges are not enough, we then use distractions as a means of being "too busy" to deal with them.

Well, let's get on with the task at hand and work through the process of managing our challenge areas.

Work through the following chart by identifying your areas for growth in the first column. In the second column, list how the challenge is affecting you. In the final column, think of ways to manage, mitigate, or eliminate these challenges.

Identify areas that you think are areas for growth or create challenges for growth.	What impact does this challenge have on your ability to achieve your goals and dreams?	What are the ways/tools/people that you engage in or leverage to manage/mitigate/eliminate these challenges?

Access full-size printable charts using the QR code on page 192

Example:

Identify areas that you think are areas for growth or create challenges for growth.	What impact does this challenge have on your ability to achieve your goals and dreams?	What are the ways/tools/people that you could engage in or leverage to manage/mitigate/eliminate these challenges?
Organization	I am often overwhelmed and feel as though I have too much to do between work and home and so everything feels like it's a mess/chaos.	Use my calendar to plan work and personal priorities. Take a couple of days off and do a massive spring cleaning at home, including my car and laptop files so that I really get organized once and for all.
Delegating/Asking Others for Help	I have trouble asking for help, but that often means I end up working very late and don't get enough sleep and get grumpy with myself and others.	I need to ask for help. I need to look at my list and see where I can give things to my partner and to people at work and let go. This will free up my time, but I need to do this so it is long term, not one-and-done.
Financial Management	I get nervous managing money and figuring out a budget so I avoid it, and therefore always feel anxious, and I don't invest in learning so that I can achieve my goals.	I could read a few books, watch some YouTube videos, and create a spreadsheet. I know there are free budgeting templates I could use. I need to do this.
Time Management	I always have a million things to do and never enough time so I don't get to work on my goals.	I need to get better at creating my schedule weekly so I can make time for achieving my goals.

The real benefit in working through your challenges is that you discover methods for mitigating or managing them. This awareness helps to build your own resilience and self-determination but also identifies areas where you need to reach out for help from others. And though we likely hate to admit it, it is when we face challenges, when we push ourselves beyond our comfort zones, that we grow.

Bottom line, when we adopt a growth mindset, we learn to see our challenges as opportunities to grow and learn, rather than as failures. There is no need to "be all things"—you can be great at a few things and lean into the greatness/strengths of others for other things.

FACTORS THAT IMPACT THE ACHIEVEMENT OF GOALS AND DREAMS

☐ Factor 4: Distractions and derailers

We live in an era of mass distraction. Distractions are everywhere, impacting us at work, home, and even while we are pursuing our biggest dreams. Distractions are the things that we do so that we don't do what we need to do! Derailers—of which distractions can be one—are things that throw us off track, like a sudden phone call or email or notification. They cause us to lose our focus or train of thought.

Each person has their own list of distractions and derailers, but let me get you started (with some of my own):

- Social media
- Notifications (from different apps advising me of things that are likely not priorities)
- Cleaning
- Organizing
- Making lists
- Eating
- Exercising
- Watching TV
- Having a bath/shower
- Getting groceries

While some of these things are necessary to sustain life, they all have a time and a place. It is when we use them as an avoidance tactic that it becomes an issue. Not sure about you, but I do this all the time: I will often tell myself that I cannot work on a project or priority until my house is clean, my laundry is away, my fridge is full, etc. I would do all these tasks anyway, but I use them as a means of keeping busy so that I don't do my real work.

Once I became aware, I began to notice when I was making excuses to not do the work I needed to do. I stopped with the excuses and got to work! So how do we become aware and then course correct ourselves—by noting the things that we do that may "waste" time or that we could do another time? We need to be aware of when we are putting something off. When we are delaying dealing with an issue or opportunity. When we are resisting something. We need to call ourselves out. We need to notice what we are avoiding, why and how we are spending (wasting/allocating) time when we could be focusing on the priority/thing we need to do versus some other less productive and/or important activity. And here is the crux of the issue when we get distracted or derailed: we slow or even halt progress, we lose sight of our priorities, and we have difficulty staying motivated. It's a downward spiral of our own creation, causing stress, anxiety, poor health, sleepless nights, and reduced work quality. You get it. The impact is significant—and avoidable.

Complete the following chart by listing your distractions/derailers in the first column, the impact they are having on your productivity, and any ways you can think of to address them.

DISTRACTIONS/DERAILERS The things that throw off your focus and stop you from focusing on the work that propels your life forward (and that you really want to do).	What impact are these distractions and derailers having on your time management and your ability to focus?	What are some ways that you can still do these things (or not) without having them get in the way of achieving your goals and dreams and doing the work you need/want to do?

Access full-size printable charts using the QR code on page 192

Example:

DISTRACTIONS/DERAILERS The things that throw off your focus and stop you from focusing on the work that propels your life forward (and that you really want to do).	What impact are these distractions and derailers having on your time management and your ability to focus?	What are some ways that you can still do these things (or not) without having them get in the way of achieving your goals and dreams and doing the work you need/want to do?
Social Media	I check my IG and FB several times an hour so I can see what everyone is doing.	I could put a time limit on viewing or limit to certain times of the day.
Cleaning the House/ Chores	I like everything to be clean and neat before I start to work. Sometimes I take this too far and over clean!	I could create a schedule for what needs to be done each day.
Going Out with Friends	I love going out with my friends. I go out several times a week and sometimes we are out late.	I could schedule my time and activities with my friends and also my priorities so that I achieve my priorities at the end of the week and still have fun.
Playing Video Games	I play video games as a way to chill and relax, but sometimes I get caught up in the game and end up spending hours playing. I lose track of times.	I could set an alarm so that I limit my playing time.

So, how do you feel after that? Do you feel like you can honestly manage distractions? I think we will always have an opportunity to do something that is more interesting, fun, or easy than what we are doing. But I can share that since doing this exercise, I recognize when I am off track. I recognize the impact, and I evaluate how much time or energy I put into the distraction. I have also noticed that when I am becoming easily distracted, it is because I need to take a break, move my body, and change my mood. There is a reason we get distracted. So when you notice the tendency rising within you, refresh yourself. Go for a walk. Get a fresh glass of water or a cup of coffee. Splash some cold water on your face. Manage the requirement to shift your focus for a few minutes and use it to your advantage.

Derailers, on the other hand, are slightly more complicated. These occur when someone else influences our mood. Yes, another person can be a distraction. But the slight differentiation with a derailer is that it can cause a complete spiral, shifting your mood from happy to sad or from sad to happy (which can be a good thing). Again, it's the awareness of the impact that someone is having on you, your physical and mental health, and your focus. Note this and decide whether it is healthy or unhealthy, and with that assess the need for boundaries. On a personal note, I am easily derailed by the mood of others—specifically, the bad or stressed mood of others. Knowing this, I create inner boundaries that help me to cope. I don't shut the person out, but I isolate the time I spend with them in order to protect my own energy. I then step away, refresh myself similar to the distractions—get fresh air, wash my face and hands—and often I do a meditation or breathing exercise. These simple efforts help me to reframe my perspective and get back on track. The cues on my phone, laptop, and wall of my vision board also help. They consistently and continuously remind me of the direction I am going and to get back on track.

Well, we have just done some pretty heavy lifting! You will be happy and/or relieved that the next two factors are super positive and will help to build your momentum before we go onto the next step in the Life Blueprint exercise.

But we have one more thing I would like you to do before we dive into these factors. **I want you to draw a proverbial "line in the sand" and leave the fears, the limiting beliefs, the distractions and the derailers that no longer serve you as you move forward, behind you. This does not mean they are gone. It does not mean that you will forget they exist/existed. It does not mean that you don't have work to do to deal with them. What it does mean is that they are no longer going to hold you back.**

Now, here is where once again, I am going to ask you to perform a ritual. You may roll your eyes at me, but trust me, these tips and tricks that I am sharing work. I am living proof of that, as are many others. No pressure, but you are here because something isn't working, right?! Or because you want something different. Or you want more. Well, give it a try. Take all the charts of "dirty work" that you have just completed and tear them up (you can make a copy if you want but put it in an envelope and put it with your files—it is for reference or as a reminder only). Then put them in a pot or urn or safe vessel, grab some matches, and go outside. In a fire safe place, light these papers on fire and let them burn. When they are nothing more than ashes and there are no sparks, blow the ashes safely into the air. **Let them go!** You are giving these fears, limiting beliefs, distractions and derailers to the Universe to manage. They are no longer going to hold you back. With this ritual, you have put a philosophical "line in the sand"—you are crossing over the line and leaving these "issues" and will forever be reminded when one of them starts to rise within you or impact you in any way that you have let them go. That you left them on the other side of the line.

I would like to tell you that this means you have dealt with them and they will never resurface. That may or may not be the case. You may have more work to do to manage and/or overcome them, and you may need or want to seek support from a therapist and/or professional. My point in following this ritual is that you have decided these issues are not going to hold you back as you move forward. You are moving on and they are not coming!

Okay, now get ready for some positive vibes!

FACTORS THAT IMPACT THE ACHIEVEMENT OF GOALS AND DREAMS

☐ Factor 5: Accomplishments

I find it so funny, but in my experience coaching thousands of individuals through this process, these last two factors—accomplishments and strengths—are often the most difficult ones for people to complete. Our fears spring to the surface easily, but our accomplishments, our strengths? It's as though I am pulling teeth!

I find it challenging that I continually have to explain that accomplishments are more than just about the accomplishment. They are opportunities to learn and grow, and they're important for motivation. They are the stepping stones for future accomplishments and therefore for the achievement of your goals. **Drawing on past accomplishments when facing new challenges builds self-assurance and confidence**. A positive attitude toward past accomplishments fuels the courage to take on new endeavors and tackle new challenges.

So, here is my ask—go back as far as you can, to when you were a child. Remember when you sang your first song, read your first book, got an A, completed a race, completed grade school, got your first job, etc. List everything!

When you take note of everything that you have accomplished, you will realize that you are stronger and more capable than you have given yourself credit for. In addition, on the days ahead when you face challenges, remembering these accomplishments will give you the strength to know you can do it.

Steve Jobs best expressed this sentiment by saying that it is not until much later in our lives when we reflect back on our experiences that we see their relevance in how our life unfolds. Our accomplishments often foster growth and confidence that we do not fully explore because we achieve and move on. Failures and challenges, on the other hand, we tend to ruminate on, look for the learnings.

In this exercise, I am asking you to take a pause and reflect. Our accomplishments are what we lean into when things get rough! This exercise may become a work in progress, and you may think of more as you progress through the Life Blueprint process, but at least get the party started. A helpful tip is to keep this chart beside your desk, so you can add to it as you remember things. In fact, I do this for all the charts.

Complete the following chart by listing your accomplishments (no matter how small!) in the first column, followed by how it makes you feel in the second column, and what learning you had from this experience and how it perhaps fueled you in other areas or as you moved forward in life, in the third column.

ACCOMPLISHMENTS List all of your accomplishments— big and small (size does not matter!)	How did this accomplishment make you feel?	What learning or benefit can you source from this accomplishment?

Access full-size printable charts using the QR code on page 192

Example:

ACCOMPLISHMENTS List all of your accomplishments— big and small (size does not matter!)	How did this accomplishment make you feel?	What learning or benefit can you source from this accomplishment?
Grade 2 Spelling Bee Winner	I was so proud because when I ran home after school and told my parents, they were so proud and we all went out for ice cream!	I learned to celebrate victories. Even small victories. And in big and small ways!
First job at 14	I got my first job as a store clerk at my local grocery store. I was so excited because my family really needed the money and I could help.	I felt like an adult. I felt like I could contribute to my family. I felt responsible.
Driver's license at 16	I was super happy when I got my driver's license. So many of my friends had failed. And I really needed and wanted to get my license because I lived far away from transit and this was going to make my life so much easier.	I learned that if I focused and practiced, I would be able to achieve a goal. I drove every day for months with my parents so that by the time I did my driving test, I was ready.
Graduated from university	I was the first person in my family to go to university, so when I graduated I was very proud of myself.	I learned that I can accomplish a big goal that spanned over many years if I focused my energy and attention. I did not love all my courses but I am so glad I finished my degree. Thanks to sticking with it I have been able to get good jobs and create a nice life for myself and my family. I proved that hard work and sticking with things can pay off.

Critical to this exercise is noting what led to the accomplishments and how to leverage the learning, strength, and resilience you demonstrated in future endeavors. Recognize the optimism and validation you feel within your body when you review your accomplishments. And remind yourself to use these accomplishments as fuel, as sources of inspiration, and as confidence boosters when you start to stray the course! While you are in this positive mindset and seeing all the things you have done so far, I want you to work through the last factor—your strengths.

FACTORS THAT IMPACT THE ACHIEVEMENT OF GOALS AND DREAMS

☐ Factor 6: Strengths

We close this step with strengths because I want you to end on a high note. I want you to see and feel your greatness. Your power. Your will. Your determination. Your resilience. You can do whatever you put your mind to, and you have proven that. **When we understand our strengths, we can harness our full potential and unlock a world of opportunities.** We come to see our innate gifts and abilities, such as creativity or empathy. We note our learned skills/capabilities through training and experience, such as critical thinking, management, cooking, public speaking, etc. In the process of developing and realizing our strengths, we gain clarity on our core values, principles, and beliefs. An awareness of our strengths shapes our optimism and sheer desire and determination to achieve our dreams.

Take a deep breath. Don't be humble! It's just you and me here. And I want you to own all your greatness and let it shine—that is why we are here.

Identify and reflect on your strengths and how they can be used in various aspects of your life. Complete the following chart by listing your strengths in the first column and how you can use them in the second column.

STRENGTHS List everything that makes you awesome. Ask yourself: What do I love about myself?	What are the ways that you could further optimize/leverage these strengths? (We often don't think about this!)

Access full-size printable charts using the QR code on page 192

Example:

STRENGTHS List everything that makes you awesome. Ask yourself: What do I love about myself?	What are the ways that you could further optimize/leverage these strengths? (We often don't think about this!)
Work Ethic	I am a really hard, focused worker. When I set my mind to something or take responsibility, I will get it done. This strength helps me get through the parts of work and projects that are not fun or are overwhelming. I know that if I set my mind to it, I can get anything done/figured out.
Very Organized	I am super organized and this allows me to prioritize projects and to-dos. I can get a lot done in a day/week because I create a list and organize my week and allocate the right amount of time to things. This has also helped me build my reputation because people know they can count on me.
Diplomacy	I am a good listener and am not afraid of tough or confrontational conversations. This means that peers often invite me into important conversations because they know I will help to create a win-win solution for everyone.
Fun Personality	I love that people think I am fun. I often get invited to things because I add some fun to the situation. This has allowed me to go to so many events and functions I would not normally have had the pleasure of attending. And because of this, I have built some great personal and professional relationships.

So, how did it go?

Reflect for a moment and take pride in your strengths and acknowledge the positive impact they have on you and others. Recognize that our strengths are a work in progress and that continuous learning and growth is a lifelong journey.

And pull out that tape!

Right now, the "taking stock" chart should be on your wall. I am going to ask you to now tape up your Accomplishments and Strengths charts. Often, as the hours/days unfold and you work through the Life Blueprint process, you will think of other accomplishments and strengths—yay! Add them to the chart. The more the merrier! These lists will continue to fuel and inspire you and are living proof that you can do whatever you set your mind to!

These accomplishments and strengths have set the bar for you. You cannot fall below this bar—it is impossible. You can only rise! Let me explain.

We do not rise to the level of our expectations. We fall to the level of our training.

–Archilochus

I first heard this quote when I watched a YouTube video where a Navy SEAL gave a commencement speech and quoted Archilochus. While there is more content and context to this quote, what I took away is that once we have created a strength within us or achieved a level of confidence, this becomes our new normal, our standard. As we move forward and face future challenges, it is at this standard where we begin or default. We cannot fall below it because we have had the experience. We have built the muscle. We cannot have had an experience and then honestly and authentically deny its existence. We can only use this experience as wisdom or learning to take with us as we move toward our next experience. And so I ask you as we start to bring this step to a close to continue to remind yourself of your strengths and accomplishments and how they can continue to serve, elevate, and fuel you as you move forward.

Well, that's a wrap for Step 2. Your groundwork has been laid! Dirty work done! Congratulations on completing what is, admittedly, the most challenging part of the process. Please be sure to release your fears, limiting beliefs, challenges, and distractions and derailers. Tape your accomplishments and strengths to the wall and take some time to review them. Having worked through each of these areas, your awareness is heightened, and you may think of more things to add to each one.

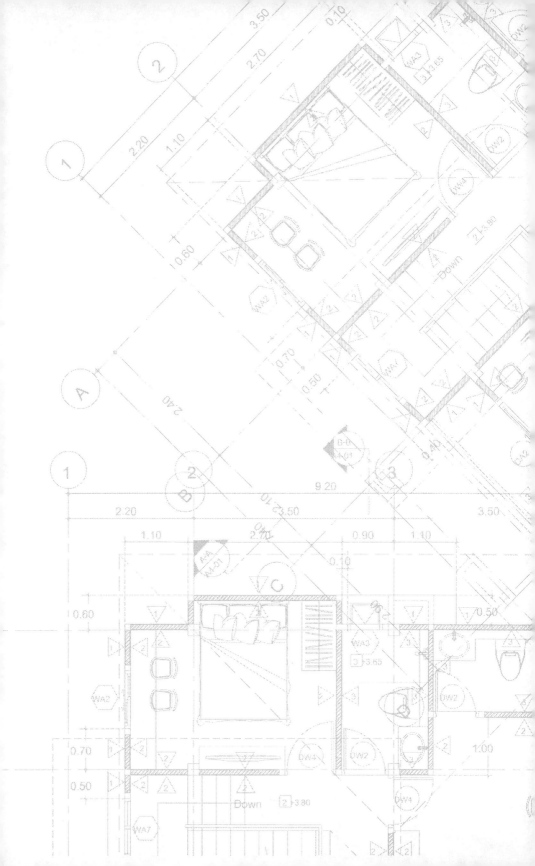

Step 3

Decide Your Legacy/Impact—Defining your dash

So you may not always have a comfortable life. And you will not always be able to solve all the world's problems all at once. But don't ever underestimate the impact you can have, because history has shown us that courage can be contagious, and hope can take on a life of its own.

–Michelle Obama

In the title for this chapter, what is the dash to which I refer? The dash is the critical line that connects our year of birth to the year of our death. It will be used on all legal and funeral documents and notices at the time of our passing. It is nothing but a simple dash, but it is perhaps one of the most complex lines we will come across in our life. The dash holds within it everything that we have ever done in our lives. There are countless stories and poems—often read at funerals—about the dash. Symbolically, it represents all that we were. For our purposes, it represents all that we want to be remembered for. The beauty of this step in the process is that it allows us to predefine the dash. To predetermine its meaning and significance and work toward making that real every day.

Leaving a positive impact on the world is a fundamental human need. Whether it is through our professional or personal life, the legacy we leave behind will undoubtedly shape future generations. In this next step, I will use the words "legacy" and "impact" somewhat interchangeably. Our legacy is the memories, values, and actions that people will associate with your name long after you are gone. Impact refers to the positive change you make in the world; the difference you make in the lives of those around you. My hope is that through this next exercise you will get clear on the legacy you want to leave behind, and therefore, the impact you want to make. As Maya Angelou reminded all of us, "Life is not measured by the number of breaths we take, but by the moments that take our breath away."

When we think about legacy and/or impact, different contexts may come to mind for each of us.

- Material legacy—Leaving material possessions behind for future generations, such as money, property, art, or other prized possessions.

- Social legacy—Shaping societal aspects such as education, justice, or health care to create positive change for future generations.

- Personal legacy—Leaving behind unique personal values, beliefs, or personality traits that positively influence those who follow in your footsteps.

The legacy we choose to leave behind and the impact it makes is unique to each and every one of us. In this exercise, we are going to explore your legacy and the effect you want to have.

I shared with you previously that my life took a rather dramatic turn when my marriage ended. When that happened, I lost my clarity and the vision I had for my legacy. The narrative I had scripted for myself and my family was gone. I was completely lost. And I needed a radical shake-up because I was spiraling, and not in a good way.

I searched everywhere for resources to help me cope, to be better at work and at home. Sure, there were books on specific issues, but nothing that was an all-in-one solution. I would get out of bed each day and seize the day—what choice did I have?—but inside I was lost. I was working around the clock, running my agency, and doing my best to raise our three teenage children in a new way with my ex-husband, while caring for a house and trying to be a reasonable leader, mom, daughter, sister, and friend. It's no surprise that I dropped more than a few balls, which of course rotted my gut and made me feel even worse. Each day was a struggle, and I knew I needed to make a change or I was going to implode. I was neither living the legacy nor having the impact I wanted to have.

I signed up for a weekend course: "48 hours to change your life." While the course was good, there was one distinct hour that did change my life. I am not being dramatic here. This next exercise changed everything for me.

Because of the effect this exercise had on me, I am reluctant to provide too much information ahead of time because I want it to have an equal or greater impact on you. So what follows are explicit directions. My ask is that you give yourself thirty to sixty minutes of alone time for this step. Unless you are going to allocate the time, energy, and focus right now, don't do it. Don't skip this step and move forward to the other ones. Make the time to do it right as it truly is a game changer and is critical in helping you create life balance and perspective.

Trusting you have the time—please read on and follow the directions. If you are ready to do it right now, please get a few blank pieces of paper, a blue pen, and your mobile device.

Directions:

- Set a timer for twenty minutes.
- Put on soft acoustic music.
- Write your eulogy and importantly NOT your obituary:
    - An obituary shares birth and death dates, family left behind, key stats with some emotion. It does not share your story.
    - Your eulogy is your story. It is what people will say about you after you die.
    - At the reception or ceremony when they celebrate your life, what will be said?
    - Write it—from the perspective of those who are celebrating your life.
- Don't think.
- Don't edit.
- Just write.

When you have completed writing your eulogy, take a break. I trust you can relate that after this exercise, there was not a dry eye at the weekend workshop I attended. Hence, the reason I need you to take a pause. Go for a walk. Get a glass of water.

When you return, reread what you wrote and ask yourself if you are living consistently every day to ensure the legacy and impact you just wrote about will actually come into fruition. Because the truth is, we could "be gone" at any moment. You need to ask yourself how will you be remembered and is that what you want? What would others say about you and what would your impact be if your "gone moment" was now?

If in your eulogy you said you hoped that your son said you were the ideal mom for him and that he knew you always had his back and loved him unconditionally—then, are you acting in a way that your son will actually say that back? If you wrote about a community impact, charitable or volunteer work that changed the lives of others—again I ask, will there be voices who note this about you? Read what you wrote and think about it right now from the perspective of the person who is saying it. Are you living up to that expectation that you have set for yourself?

I don't mean to apply huge pressure here. But if this is the legacy and impact you want to leave behind and you are not consistently delivering this, then consider making some changes.

Take it all in. Absorb what you wrote. Absorb the legacy you want to leave. How amazing are all the memories that you want people to have? And most importantly, how you made them feel.

Our legacy is all about "the breaths we take away," the moments and memories we create.

And to that point, continue to ponder whether you are living in a way that reflects the legacy you want to leave behind.

This question was the most powerful and game-changing one I have ever been asked. "Was I living in a way that would yield the eulogy I wanted?" Honestly, I was not living in a way that was consistent with my eulogy.

I took the weekend course and did this exercise seven years after my separation. During that time, I certainly had a ton of ups and downs. A self-diagnosed Type A, anxious and neurotic female, I dragged myself, my children, and my colleagues through a ton of shit. I lived stressed, sleepless, and ever-demanding of myself and those in my circle. Certainly I was generous and supportive, but I was also hyper intense. This exercise stopped me cold.

I remember calling my oldest child and crying. Overwhelmed and very apologetic, I committed to "do better because I now know better" (to paraphrase Maya Angelou). I made a lot of apologies after that weekend.

I changed. And I continue to change and use the legacy exercise as my litmus test for how I live, how I will be remembered, and the impact that I want to have. And now, I ask myself daily if I am living the way I want to be remembered. I would like to tell you that I have lived flawlessly since that day of reckoning, but that would be a lie. I took the course in 2013—it made some of my regrets pre-2013 bigger, and it has made any falterings since then more gut-wrenching. And I have faltered. Not intentional but failings nonetheless. I work hard every day to be better and do better.

So, I ask you, are you living in alignment with your eulogy? Have the honest conversation with yourself. Note the changes you need to make and make them. Start now. And continue to ask yourself this question every day. We don't know when our last day will present itself.

The eulogy exercise is critical to ensuring that as you create a plan that propels you toward the achievement of your vision(s), you do so in harmony with the legacy you want to leave. These two must be in sync for your life to be in harmony.

Very importantly, and I must stress this, the critical goal of the legacy/impact exercise is to ground yourself in the present. Read that again. **The critical goal of the legacy/impact exercise is to ground yourself in the present. It is critical that you live each day the way you want to be remembered.**

Read what you wrote again and ask yourself—are you living so that if something were to happen to you (sorry to write this, but I need to make the point), you would be remembered the way you are hoping for? And what can you do to ensure this? How can you alter your daily practices, interactions, and ways of living and working to be consistent with your legacy and the impact you want to have?

I invite you to take some time right now to think about some changes you could make every day so that your legacy is real. Put plans in place so that you **"take breaths away, every day."**

I would suggest you take a break after this step. Go for a walk. Do some stretches. Call your mom or your kids. Give yourself a hug. We truly don't know how many days we have left. All we know is that we have the moment we are in, so our goal needs to be to live true to our vision, mission, values, and legacy in the moments we have.

Give yourself some time to digest the work you just did. Then tape it to your wall alongside your other pages. We are assembling everything together piece by piece—and this was another critical piece.

Step 4

Define Your Values—The foundation upon which everything rests

If you have built castles in the air, your work need not be lost; that is where they should be. Now put foundations under them.

–Henry David Thoreau

It is no secret that I did not enjoy university. Don't get me wrong, I loved and still love learning, and I often consider going back to school. I love the hallowed halls of academia and cerebral life conversations. What I struggled with was the rigor of courses and assignments that seemed to serve no purpose taught by people who were often disinterested. I loved Philosophy and Humanities—electives, not mandatory courses, chosen to enrich/broaden our thinking. I always found these profs to be the most engaged, enlightened, and passionate. And it was in one of these courses that I read Thoreau's book *Walden*. Though there are many life lessons in the book, the one that has impacted my life more than any other was the passage quoted above. For me, a solid foundation—be it physical or philosophical—is fundamental to the decisions we make. Foundations are the basis for success. And values are our foundation. They are the guiding principle that shape our lives. Leaning into the house analogy—they are the foundation upon which the house is built.

It was from the quote that opens this step and the interception of the concepts of foundations and structures, both mental and physical, that gave birth to naming this process Life Blueprint. As you know, blueprints are designs for building homes, spaces. Once there is an understanding of the topography of the land and its ability to hold a structure, the drawings begin with the "footings" and the "foundation."

We will talk about "footings" (a.k.a. key factors for success) and their role in the Life Blueprint process in another step. Right now, we are going to focus on the foundation. The foundation is the entire base upon which the structure is built. It supports everything. As an analogy, the foundation in the Life Blueprint process is our values. Our values are at the root of who we are, what we stand for, our goals and dreams, and how we live every day. Our values are ultimately what define us and guide us. They guide every decision we make—purposeful or spontaneous. And they are the truest reflection of our character.

Yet "value" is such an elusive word interpreted by each one of us uniquely. Hence, the reason this exercise is so important. We can identify our values by reflecting on what is important to us, what we stand for, what motivates us, and what brings us joy. But the challenge is that while we may all use the same word, it often comes to life for each of us differently. Here is the thing with values that I have come to discover: Often we feel comfortable or uncomfortable in certain environments or with certain people or organizations because of a connection or disconnection between them and our own values. I have even found that we may use the same words to identify the values that are most important to each of us and yet there is still a disconnection. The reason for the disconnection comes when you peel back the layers of understanding, when you take the time to share your definition of the value and how it shows up in your life. This understanding is critical. This work and/or next level of understanding is where you discover if in fact you are on the same page. If you are in fact aligned.

I have entered into several partnerships where in the initial meetings and conversations the vibe felt healthy and engaging as though something longer term seemed inevitable and risk free. Yet as the partnership unfolded, our definitions of our values—what the words mean to us—were different. And how these values showed up in our lives were even more different.

Spotting complete value misalignment or lack of fit feels evident when it is completely off. You can sense it the minute you walk into a room or shake a person's hand or make eye contact. But where there is positive energy and attraction, it still takes time to ensure there is a sustainable future based on value alignment.

Can you build a house that can weather a storm—be this personally or professionally? Will you and your life partner make similar choices as you navigate the ups and downs of life? And professionally, does your organization manage people, issues, and opportunities consistent with your thinking and way of living—consistent with your values?

Exercise:

To clarify your own values, what follows is a starter, though not all-inclusive, list of values. Read and review them, then select the top three to five that are the most important to you. From there, complete the chart provided. Consider what drives you, what is most important to you, and what makes you feel fulfilled. Identify your top values. Select values that are most essential to you. **Identifying your values is not enough; it is putting them into action that matters.**

Acceptance	Efficiency	Integrity	Punctuality
Achievement	Elegance	Intelligence	Purpose
Adaptability	Eloquence	Joy	Recognition
Adventure	Empathy	Justice	Relaxation
Ambition	Enthusiasm	Kindness	Reliability
Authenticity	Equality	Knowledge	Respect
Balance	Ethics	Leadership	Responsibility
Boldness	Family	Logic	Romance
Bravery	Fidelity	Love	Satisfaction
Calmness	Flexibility	Loyalty	Security
Charity	Freedom	Maturity	Serenity
Comfort	Generosity	Moderation	Simplicity
Commitment	Gratitude	Objectivity	Social connection
Common sense	Happiness	Optimism	Spirituality
Communication	Hard work	Originality	Success
Community	Health	Passion	Sympathy
Compassion	Helpfulness	Patience	Teamwork
Confidence	Honesty	Peacefulness	Thoughtfulness
Connection	Humility	Performance	Tolerance
Creativity	Humor	Perseverance	Tradition
Curiosity	Idealism	Pleasure	Trust
Decency	Imagination	Popularity	Truth
Dedication	Independence	Positivity	Uniqueness
Dependability	Individualism	Power	Unity
Determination	Influence	Practicality	Variety
Devotion	Innovation	Professionalism	Wealth
Education	Inspiration	Prosperity	Wisdom

Now that you have selected your top three to five values, list them below. Then, define them for yourself, in your own words. Not the dictionary or Wikipedia definition but YOUR own definition. This is important because in defining the value in your own words, you become clear on what it means to you specifically. Next, identify how you live this value. How does this value show up in your life? To make this even clearer, identify an example of how this value shows up in your life. Perhaps even take it one step further and provide an example of how you intend to demonstrate and/or reflect this value in your life moving forward. This is especially powerful and relevant after having completed the legacy/eulogy exercise. The legacy exercise brings us very much into the present moment and what really matters to us. What comes up during that exercise are your values. Lean into that exercise as you do the work on your values. How will you live this value . . . every day?

Value	How YOU define this value	How this value shows up in your life. Provide an example.	Moving forward, how you will reflect this value in your life.

Access full-size printable charts using the QR code on page 192

THE IMPACT OF LIVING BY OUR VALUES—
THREE KEY IMPACTS:

Authenticity—Living by our values promotes authenticity, which enhances self-awareness, self-acceptance, and meaningful relationships.

Focus—Living a values-driven life clarifies our priorities and reduces distractions, which increases focus, productivity, and satisfaction.

Resilience—Living by our values strengthens our resilience, which enables us to bounce back from challenges, adapt to changes, and grow from setbacks.

The thing with our values is that they are challenged daily. There are external pressures—social norms, peer pressure, and media influence—that can tempt us to compromise them. We have our own internal conflicts—misaligned values, unmet needs, and limiting beliefs—that can create internal tension and self-doubt. And there are moral gray zones—complex situations that involve trade-offs, uncertainties, and ethical dilemmas—that can challenge our values.

I hope this exercise was valuable. You just solidified your foundation!

Let's do a check-in. In keeping with the analogy of blueprints and designing a house, let me connect them.

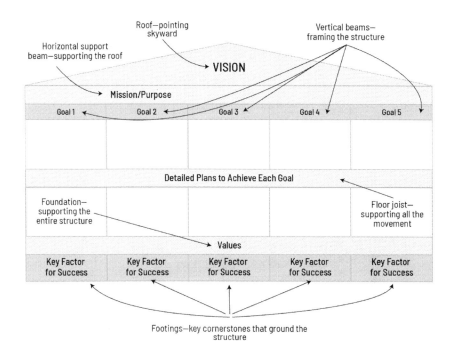

The roof represents your vision

While on a practical level the roof on a house defines the space, it provides context, shelter and security, philosophically it holds and inspires our ever-evolving growth in a safe space.

The "vision" we created in Step 1 reminds and inspires us daily to keep moving in the direction of our dreams—to seize the day!

The horizontal beam(s) represent your mission/purpose

Beams are a critical structural component. They provide support and stability and are essential for the integrity of a house just as our mission/purpose is vital for a meaningful existence.

The vertical beams represent your goals

Within a home the vertical beams provide both structural support and separation. This is analogous to the role our goals play in helping to achieve our vision. We often have three to five key goals we are focusing on at any one time. They are unique from each other but are connected by their combined effort to leverage our mission daily to achieve our vision.

The floor joists represent your plans

Floor joists allow us to create rooms and spaces on a solid base/level. Their strength and configuration allow us to "renovate" areas as our needs and/or desires change. Relative to plans that similarly can shift and evolve as goals are achieved or challenges and opportunities arise.

The foundation represents your values

Secured by footings, a foundation is the starting point upon which we build all structures. Relative to our lives, our values are the moral and ethical principles that ground our life and all our choices.

The footings represent key factors for success

Footings are the cornerstones in structures providing further stability and grounding for the foundation. Relative to the Life Blueprint, footings represent key factors for success. These are typically three to five practices that help to keep us on track when shit happens!

I am hoping the analogy of a house and blueprints is coming together for you as you work through the Life Blueprint process.

....

If you don't build castles in the air,
you won't build anything on the ground.

–Victor Hugo

....

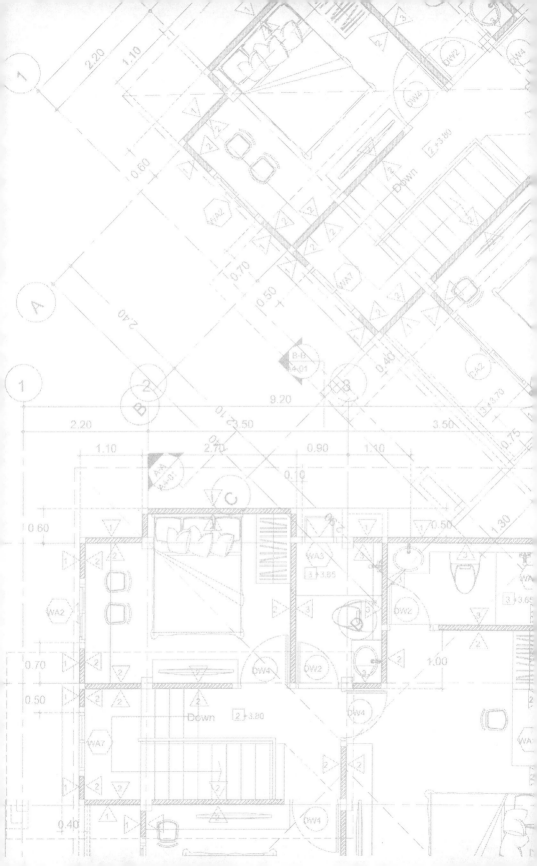

Step 5

Clarify Your Mission/Purpose—
Resolve your reason for being

Want to go on a trip?

I bet you didn't expect me to ask you this question in the middle of the book. If I could give away a free trip with each book, that would be awesome. Unrealistic and probably heart-attack–inducing for my publisher, but awesome for you (and me!). In the spirit of heart-attack management, let me take you on a virtual trip. I'm going to do my best to transport you several thousand miles away to Okinawa, Japan. Before I "transport" you to Okinawa, I want to explain why this part of the process is so important—likely one of the most important parts to you—and why it is in the middle of the Life Blueprint process.

When people reach out to me, this is almost always where they want our work together to begin. I give them a few minutes to share what is going on in their head, their struggles, their angst, their need to know, then I nudge them toward following the step-by-step Life Blueprint process. Note that your purpose is Step 5, not Step 1.

We need to do the work that precedes our purpose in order to understand both what got us to this point and where we want to go. Layer on this our legacy and values and then we have a clear picture of all the parameters in our life. There is a method to my methodology.

Years ago, when my marriage dissolved and changed our family dynamic forever, it was the shattering of my role and purpose that had the most devastating effect on me. I thought my purpose was to be a wife and mother and create this amazing life for my family and friend circle. In the unraveling of our marriage, I came completely undone! To put myself and my life back together, I had to go back to what got me to this point, to my strengths and my accomplishments. I had to do all the work that you have done to this point and then I needed to reevaluate my purpose.

I wanted to be a mom from the time I was a teenager. I wanted to create a "perfect" family life. My own childhood had gone from what I perceived as idyllic to tumultuous and disastrous. I wanted the fairy tale, and I was determined to get it. I set the course, off I went, and I achieved it! Marriage to my high school sweetheart, three children, a beautiful home, a great job, family and friends close by—I was the luckiest girl in the world. When I turned forty, I was able to look at myself and feel proud in the acknowledgment that I had done it. I had achieved the goal. The peace and satisfaction welled up inside me. To be clear, my life was far from perfect—but I was okay with the imperfections. Life was good. I was good. We were good.

And then, as I have previously shared, I wasn't good at all. Life has its challenges—this was not my first life-altering challenge, nor would it be the last.

Prior to everything coming undone, I was truly in love with my life, and I did not take it for granted. I'd had sufficient challenges up to this point to know that in a moment's notice everything could change. The dissolution of my marriage, though, was particularly life changing because we had made the fairy tale happen and then we broke it and broke ourselves. In the breaking, I was overcome with sadness, fear, and anxiety. I became frenetic, neurotic, and driven. I was determined to recreate the life I had envisioned and promised myself and had wanted for my children before they were even conceived!

And so I did. I worked crazy hours balancing the desire to be a great mom and a great business leader while managing a home and rebuilding our lives. Now almost two decades later, if I could mentor my younger self, I would hug her, slow her down, pull her away from the day-to-day, teach her to breathe, and give her the wisdom and support she so greatly needed. I would provide the guiding hand I mentioned earlier.

The guiding hand I needed then is what led to the Life Blueprint. I needed answers. I needed a path—and I still do. In business, we continuously follow paths and processes to mitigate challenges and do our best to ensure positive results. Just as in building a house, we have a set of blueprints. I needed this in my personal life, in my "whole" life. I needed a holistic plan. So I created one and started to rebuild, redefine, and envision a new version of the realistic "happily ever after" life I wanted—obviously different from the one I had before but certainly building on the good, as well as the responsibilities that remained, with a less idealistic perspective. Witnesses to the changes and positive growth asked what I was doing, and so I started to share how I was rebuilding, redefining, and recreating my life. Interested to see if my process would also work for them, they tested it out, and they started changing their lives and achieving their goals and dreams. The process was working for all of us!

The Life Blueprint process provides clarity and focus—both of which are greatly needed continuously through life. While these are the crux of the process and vision, values, legacy, and goals are critical, it is purpose that "fills our cup" and motivates us to get out of bed in the morning. **When we have purpose, we tap into our passions; we serve and we are fulfilled. We rise because we are needed, and in providing the need (a.k.a. serving others with our unique abilities), we are fulfilled.**

When my family life changed, my ways and means of serving, my passions, and my pleasures were (all in my mind) gone. No one, no coach, no friend, no mentor, no book, no course could provide me with direction or solutions to regain my footing and forge a new path. We are not given the tools to create a path, to create a life, to fulfill our dreams. It's as though we are dropped in the middle of a frantic intersection, with no traffic lights or map, and told to figure it out on our own. And just when you think you are on the edge of figuring it out, there is a sudden shift/change/crash. Whoosh!

I can tell you I have faced many, many challenges in life and as a shift/change/crash survivor, it is figure-out-able, it is survivable, and it does not have to be so difficult. I was so (naively) positive when I headed into my twenties and started to create my family. I had no idea what was in store. I did not realize the magnitude of continuous change in life. I thought that if I stuck to my dreams, did my part, and was genuinely grateful, then life would continue "happily ever after."

I don't want to be a downer; I want to be realistic. "Happily ever after" can and does exist. But it may not be constant. It may last for moments or perhaps days, but it is rarely if ever consistent every minute of every day. Perhaps we need to reframe life, reframe the role of happiness and expectations. Life is a journey with ups and downs—we know this. The ups and downs will continue whether we like them or not. But with a blueprint to fall back on, we have a path when the going gets tough. Sure, we may make changes, but we have a point from which to make these changes. We have put a stake in the ground and are not directionless. With our vision and legacy as guiding lights, and our values grounding us, we can move forward and choose to adjust as required. This is powerful when times are tough, and equally powerful when times are amazing. We are reminded to stay the course because it's working!

When we live in sync with our purpose, getting out of bed is easy. Trust me on this. We don't complain about work because we feel the value of our work in our core. We don't even call it work anymore. It becomes our calling. It becomes how we serve. It becomes our magic.

While I do think we are all born with a magical purpose and that we are put on this earth to have an impact, I also think that our magic and purpose evolves as we evolve. Our purpose in our twenties is different from that of our thirties, forties, fifties, and beyond. We are very much the sum of our history, and it is in the living that we clarify and evolve our purpose. Some of us may launch a mission to change the world at a young age like Greta Thunberg, while others may not embrace and share until much later. I think we often delay embracing our purpose for a few reasons:

1. We are provided with a template for living by our family and/or those around us, and we follow the plan. There are expectations and to not follow these would be unacceptable, disrespectful. You know what I mean. So we follow the path we are told to follow. Then at some point, we choose to break free and follow our inner voice because its volume and energy has become so loud we can no longer ignore it or push it to the side. We need to listen and see where it takes us.

2. We give fear the power to keep us in our place, to live in our comfort zone. In our minds, fear keeps us safe. But does it? When we live in fear, we do not live fully. And ultimately, we may live our lives never having fully explored our own amazingness, let alone that of the world.

3. We have created a life with accountabilities and responsibilities and now venturing onto a new path feels irresponsible, ungrateful of our current life, or too much work to change.

4. We just don't know what we don't know, and we need help figuring it out.

5. The trajectory of our life just hit a big, unexpected bump—good or bad—that has thrown you for a loop and now the way forward is blurry.

And you may have other reasons beyond those just listed. Think through your reasons. We peeled back several layers in Step 2 when we did the "dirty work," but this is a never-ending process. There is "always something," and it is important that we are consciously aware at all times of why we don't take action or stay on track. Ultimately, we all need to continuously deal with the haunting voices, niggling feelings inside that wants . . . more, better. And we need to put the things that hold us back behind the "line in the sand" so we can move forward. Failing to "deal" will cause us angst. I am speaking from strong personal experience when I share this. Dealing with my "demons" and figuring out my purpose was the driving force behind creating the Life Blueprint process. Thankfully, we have done the "dirty work" and have afforded ourselves the opportunity to go on an adventure. So, buckle up and let's head to Okinawa.

WELCOME TO OKINAWA!

Comprised of 160 islands, Okinawa is a "blue zone" (go to my website for books on blue zones if you are interested in learning more) boasting the highest concentration of people living over 100 years of age. Okinawans spend 97 percent of their lives, on average, free of any disabilities. They don't diet—they eat fresh, farm-picked produce every day. They don't exercise because movement is part of their life—gyms are underutilized. They meditate and have very strong faith. They also have strong social networks.

Okinawa is also the home of *ikigai*, which means life's worth and/ or life's mission. *Ikigai* is fundamental to the health and well-being of the Okinawans. The concept of *ikigai* has been around for centuries in Japan, originating from ancient philosophies such as Confucianism and Taoism. The people of Okinawa, Japan, have embraced the concept of *ikigai* and attribute it to their healthy and happy lives. They see *ikigai* (purpose) as the pursuit of doing something that you love, that serves those you love. This keeps you focused, happy, and healthy. *Ikigai* is about really understanding your life's worth and your purpose. It gets to the root of how individual purpose and passion are fundamental to the success of these communities. Everyone understands their purposes and in relation to everyone else. They come together as a community, then they divide and conquer, leaning into and onto each other's unique strengths. They complement versus compete with one another, which is obviously a beautiful way to live in the spirit of understanding. The Okinawans have tried to explain the *ikigai*

model by illustrating it through a series of concentric circles, with the convergence of these circles being areas where individuals identify their value to the community and therefore their purpose.

I have taught this methodology several times to North Americans and find it a bit challenging because we are typically less communal and more siloed in how we operate. We don't come together as an entire community to manage food, clothing, education, or other requirements, and then divide and conquer the management of these needs by leveraging one another's strengths. We operate far more independently. That said, I have leveraged key attributes of *ikigai* thinking and the methodology created a model that has proven to be very successful for people and helps them to discover and/or unlock their purpose and potential.

I separated the circles into columns, and I ask everyone to look at each section separately. Work through each one individually without even considering the others. This is another great exercise to do and then tape the chart to the wall because there are always builds and/or additions that happen as you continue to ponder. And there are also always revelations.

Start by thinking about all the things you love to do. The things that make you happy, that energize and fuel you and make your heart sing. Do you love to garden? Do you love to sit out in the sun? Do you love to read? Do you love to cook? Do you love to fish? Do you love to draw buildings? What are all the things you love to do? It's really important that you actually go from the sublime to the ridiculous when you make your list because when I give you the example of an awareness one of my students of this program had, you're going to go "Oh my God, that's ridiculous—and now it's sublime!"

What do I love to do?

Access full-size
printable charts
using the QR code
on page 192

Certainly, there are LOTS of things you are good at. Again, think of the smallest to the largest examples. Here are some thought-starters: cleaning, organizing, gardening, washing the car, fixing things, writing, listening, cooking, photography. List everything and refer to the accomplishments and strengths charts you previously completed for further inspiration.

What am I good at?

Access full-size
printable charts
using the QR code
on page 192

We can be paid for LOTS of things—every one of the examples listed is being offered by someone for remuneration. So think through what you can be paid for. You will be amazed at what you will come up with.

What can I be paid for?

Access full-size
printable charts
using the QR code
on page 192

We all know the world needs lots of things. You are welcome to list these. However, what I would really like you to focus on is what the world needs relative to what matters to you and to the things you would like to impact.

What does the world need?

·····························

**Access full-size
printable charts
using the QR code
on page 192**

·····························

Before you "think you are finished," once again refer to the other charts you have completed/taped to the wall and see if they trigger any other ideas. Also replay previous conversations with family, friends, and colleagues. When do they reach out to you for help and advice? Thinking about these conversations, when do you get excited when you are sharing something with them? Chances are you are talking about something you love to do or are good at!

When you have completed the four columns separately and you think you have exhausted every possibility, take a step away. Go for yet another walk, freshen your perspective, then come back and look at the columns. Place them side by side.

What do I love to do?	What am I good at?	What can I be paid for?	What does the world need?

Access full-size printable charts using the QR code on page 192

I always ask everyone to stand up when they review the four columns. Lay them down on a flat surface and look at them. I feel like this aerial view gives you a different perspective. **When you** *change* **your perspective, you change your** *perspective.*

Peer down and ponder the four columns; start to note the potential connections between them. What I want and am hoping you will now see are connections and possibilities that you have not seen or noticed before in your life. Opportunities to note where passions may connect to opportunities to be paid. Passions tend to be a connection between what you love to do and what you're good at. An ideal workday occurs when we get paid for work that we love to do. You know that proverb: "Choose a job you love and you'll never have to work a day in your life." My goal is to help you get there, so look at the charts!

Let me give you an example that may help. Keep in mind as I share this story that I have taken people spanning from age fifteen to seventy-two through the Life Blueprint process. (Yup, you read that correctly—seventy-two!)

Remember my point earlier about "sublime to ridiculous"? My example is from a nineteen-year-old student who was taking one of my marketing classes. Her intent in the course was to develop her skills and work in the creative department of an agency and eventually become a creative director. At nineteen, she was frustrated because she lacked the experience and exposure to get even a part-time job in her field of study. As the term was coming to a close, she was on the hunt for a summer job, and though she was sending out résumés and applying everywhere, she was getting a ton of declines. She was pretty demotivated, which made her become even more introverted and reclusive than normal. She loved gaming, and as a result, she started spending an inordinate amount of time at her console—causing concern for both her mom and her brother. Increasingly, the conversation over upcoming tuition payments added to her stress. While stressing, she remembered the Life Blueprint process I had assigned in class, and she pulled up the *ikigai* exercise on her screen.

I went back to my ikigai exercise, and I was like okay, where can I make money? And hopefully not be miserable?! I printed out the chart, put it on my bed, and stared down at it. After about five minutes, I remembered a conversation I had yesterday with one of the gamers I was talking to online—and suddenly, ding-ding-ding—it all started to come together! I had the answer to my problem right in front of me.

In her very first column, she noted her love for gaming. Her love was multifold—it was competitive (and she was good at it), it provided an escape from the tumultuous home in which she lived, and she was part of an online community where her talent was noticed, respected, and sought after. In her gaming world, she had created an amazing avatar for herself. Now, I'm not a gamer, so I don't really get the whole point of an avatar, but apparently hers was extraordinary. It had the "bells and whistles" and visuals and sounds and everything that people in the gaming world notice. Other gamers started to comment on her avatar and asked her for help creating theirs. However, not all of them could achieve the same level of creativity that she had achieved, so some asked if she would make avatars for them and they would pay her. Are you starting to see the point of this story?!

This student never really thought her love of gaming would ever connect to creating an income—but it did. Other gamers started to offer her money, and slowly but surely, she turned her passion into a highly pleasurable and rewarding income stream. She was doing work she loved and was good at it. She was able to generate an income and people needed her to do this for them because they didn't have the time or capability to do it for themselves. She found a connection among the columns that allowed her to serve and be served!

I am also sharing this example because often when we do exercises like this, we give ourselves the unnecessary expectation of having to do "noble work" for a "noble cause." We apply judgment. But I ask you is there anything more noble than doing something that makes you and others happy? My student now has an avatar development business!

Oh my God, people get so excited when I deliver them their avatar. And I always add in something that they never expect. I love their reactions!

So, go back to your aerial view and start to connect the dots. And as you do so, please remove the shackles of expectation and judgment.

Another inspiring example is someone I worked with whose job in financial services absolutely did not fill her soul, but she loved to cook. She was often sharing her recipes online, from decadent broccoli brownies (a desperate plea to get her kids to eat vegetables) to delicious baked pasta dishes, and she decided to put them all together in a hardcover cookbook. She also developed a series of e-cookbooks!

She is happier than ever because this other part of her life—her passion for cooking—is fulfilling her while serving others. She is still working her banking job, but her perspective of her job has changed. It provides a steady income and a solid group of colleagues to test her recipes on.

Everyone at work loves Monday mornings. I do most of my recipe development on the weekends when we have guests over, and I always make too much food. My guests always say everything is great—because they are my guests! But my colleagues at work know better. They know I want objective opinions on taste and texture.

Use my added notes on this diagram to find some connective correlations. Where what you love and what you are good at converge, you will find your passion. Note here if you see your passion shining through in what you really love doing and you know you are good at!

What do I love to do?	What am I good at?	What can I be paid for?	What does the world need?
	Find your passion here	Find work that you enjoy and can get paid for here	Does the work you enjoy help others/ help the world?

↑   *Can you see a connection?*   ↑

Where what you are good at and what you can be paid for con-verge speaks to the cliché—when you love your job, you won't work a day in your life! What is bubbling up for you in the connection between those two columns?

At the intersection of work you can be paid for and what the world needs, you will transition from work that sustains you to work that serves—which is the ultimate goal. Reflect on those columns and see what you notice.

Now all of this may not be apparent at first, second, or even third glance. This is important work, and you need to really reflect on each column and then their interconnectedness. As you start to connect the columns, it is important that you try to clarify your purpose. This clarity will provide critical focus as we work through the final stages of the Life Blueprint process and ensure integration.

Going back to my banking/cookbook writer example, whether this passion will become a sustaining career is unknown. But that is not her purpose right now.

My purpose right now is to raise my children according to principles that are important to my husband and me. In the process, I also want to continue to develop myself and my creativity. My cooking fills my cup because I get to serve food to other loved ones, enhance my recipes by getting feedback from my peers, and sell my best recipes online earning an income that I then invest back into adventures and experiences that I enjoy with my family. It's a win for everyone! Right now, this works for everyone; maybe in a few years, I might want to create a YouTube series or start teaching classes. But for now, I am happy and fulfilled!

As you work through the exercise yourself, it would be great if you could craft a purpose statement for yourself similar to the one above. Attempt to try to pull together a statement that explains your mission. Clunky or eloquent, it matters not at this point. It just matters that you write something down.

An example of mine is: *My mission is to share the Life Blueprint process with as many people as possible in the hopes that I can help them create extraordinary lives.*

Think of this statement as your elevator pitch to yourself. If you met yourself, how would you clearly and succinctly introduce yourself and explain your mission/purpose? Remember the goal here is to feel fulfilled with how you are spending your time. It is also very, very important to remember that your purpose NOW will likely NOT be the same five or ten years from now. It is your purpose for this point in time. If you reflected back five or ten years ago, your purpose was very likely different than it is today. In the case of my banking/cookbook writer, her purpose ten years ago was to complete her education and begin her career. Your purpose changes and evolves as you change and evolve.

When I was twenty-five, the Life Blueprint process that I have created was not even on my radar. What was on my radar was teaching and writing and speaking. Today, I lean into these skills, and my purpose now is to encourage as many people in the world as possible to work through the Life Blueprint process because I truly believe it is a life game changer! In my midtwenties, I had neither the experience nor the wisdom to create this process. Today, at this age and stage, it is my passion and vocation!

And ten years from now, who knows? My plan is to evolve the process for entrepreneurs, for youth, for developing countries—and to adapt the process to be more in sync with other target audiences who are asking for it, as well as those who I think would benefit from it. For now, completing this book and spreading the word is my focus.

When we're purpose driven, our actions are more likely to align with success. You will get out of bed in the morning motivated to move in the direction of your vision and legacy because you will be doing so by fulfilling your purpose. When you are serving, you are likely doing work you love, and the whole process becomes fulfilling, inspiring, and purpose filled. That is the icing on the proverbial cake!

Before we move on, I want to reiterate the point that **your purpose will likely evolve as you evolve.** As we move through life, gain new learning, and enjoy new experiences, we grow—and as such, our purpose expands and evolves. **The beauty of this process is that today as you complete this for the first time,**

you are putting an important "stake in the ground," and now as you move forward, you can iterate as you grow!

With this work complete, we can work on creating a list of goals that are going to make everything we have been working through feasible. Our next step is to connect your vision, values, legacy/impact, and mission/purpose by creating an action plan that brings them all together.

Step 6

Set Measurable/Tangible Goals—
Get clear on what you want to achieve

Become a goal digger!

You are now at the stage where you have completed your vision board, which ideally encapsulates the BIG PICTURE dreams and goals that you have for your life. The vision exercise is essentially this amazing extrapolation of our goals.

The legacy exercise brings us down to earth and identifies what is really important to us and how to live every day. And we've talked about our values. Since our goals are the way we will bring our vision to life, the next step is to fit them into this process.

Goals give us tangible objectives to work toward, with milestones along the way. In order to work through this goal step thoroughly, I am going to ask you to start off by listing all your goals.

Don't evaluate. Don't judge. Don't question.

Just keep writing until you can't. And even then, tape the list to the wall so you can keep adding to it. In fact, I keep a goal list on my phone. I do this because I often think about new things I want to try and/or to achieve. By maintaining the list, I am always ready the next time I want to do some planning.

It is actually the milestones attached that allow for all of this to come together fluidly, and that can feel a little overwhelming when you say it that way. But when you start to break it down into pieces, you can see how it can become achievable; breaking your goal(s) down into pieces is fundamental, so the first step that I ask everybody to do is just the green column, where you'll list every single goal that you have. Again, this goes from the sublime to the ridiculous, so it could be learning how to scuba dive and it could be building a start-up; whatever it is, I ask you to list every single goal you have.

In addition, you have completed your legacy/eulogy exercise, which is intended to keep you on point as you work toward your goals. Your eulogy and your values should be in alignment, and together they should provide you with direction as you face challenges. Your purpose/mission has also been clarified at this point in your life and is now guiding your daily activities and ensuring you work toward your vision.

The next step is to work through your goals. The work we have done to this point has certainly been entrenched in goals, we just have not clearly identified them all. This is the work we are going to do now. As we do this "work," I want to give you a perspective on goals: "Goals are not to get but to grow." These are wise words from the self-help speaker, author, and educator Bob Proctor. **Goals are not an end destination but rather proof that when we set our minds to something we can achieve it. It is in achieving that we build our confidence, resilience, knowledge, and self-awareness. It is from the achievement of one goal that we build strength and move on to the next**. As such, goals are critical to our lives. They keep us moving, and that is perhaps the most important reason of all.

While articles and conversations abound on the link between goal achievement and mental health and well-being, an academic study by Chinese researchers Wang, Li, and Sun, et al. was published in December 2017 formally proving the connection. **The surest way to enhance your mental health and well-being is to keep moving forward toward a goal.** As I make this point, I want to remind you of your professional work and business planning. When doing planning, we set both long-term and short-term (annual) objectives. We don't question the process; we know it is critical to the health and well-being of the company. There is a diligence to the corporate goal-setting process. We do an analysis that evaluates market conditions (business review), and from there we determine what is required to create a healthy organization—from human resources and people development to operations planning to gaining competitive advantage. Doing this is second nature to all of us. In fact, it is expected. Doing less than a thorough business review and creating a formal plan for the year(s) ahead is standard business practice. Yet in our personal lives, we often do not apply this diligence. We list our goals as we head into a new year or at different points in our lives and then trust they will come to fruition without applying a critical plan to them. I'm not sure why it isn't second nature for us to lay out a plan for the achievement of our goals in our personal lives. In my opinion, it needs to become second nature.

In the process ahead, you will see that clearly understanding, evaluating, and planning your goal will not only keep you on track and inspired to achieve it, but you will also achieve it faster!

I am continuously surprised and delighted by the number of students who reconnect with me months and years after the Life Blueprint process to share that they accomplished their goal(s) ahead of plan and are happier and healthier than the outcome they expected. When you create the plan to achieve a goal and then you do the check-ins that we will discuss in Step 7, you also fine-tune your goal and the milestones. You are reminded of the impact that your achievement will have. You often learn new things along the journey and apply them to your goal—again, making the process smoother and faster.

In the case of students who have leveraged the Life Blueprint process, many of the successes relate to the achievement of professional and health goals. Here are some comments from a student:

When I first committed to the Life Blueprint process, I was unhappy at work and was debating whether to quit my job or start a side hustle. At the time, I decided to do neither. After working through the process, I decided to take some courses. While taking the courses, I started to meet other people and had new and interesting conversations. I was drawn to some Eastern Medicine practices and very specifically, some natural healing practices. As such, I took a Reiki course and am now a Reiki Master. This has greatly impacted my own health and well-being.

Today, I am still working for the same company, but my role has changed dramatically. I have shifted from Sales to Business Development. I mentor several of the new and younger employees, and I practice Reiki on certain evenings and weekends according to my own personal schedule. I have found a balance and perspective and peace in my life that I never expected. I do think that eventually I will shift to doing more Reiki and working less in my corporate career, but for now, I am really happy. I am continuing to learn and grow new practices while also taking leadership development training at work. Right now, my purpose is to continue to learn and grow myself and share this learning with others. My goals for the year ahead include the completion of a couple of courses and integration of the learning into my life and work. My friends and family have noticed a change in my personality and behavior. They have noticed that I seem calmer, happier, and healthier—because I am!

With this example and the thinking and awareness of the work we have done so far, let's move on to clarifying all of your goals and then create a plan to achieve them. The first part is super easy. All you need to do is list all the goals you can think of. Write them ALL down. Every last one.

Goal	Goal	Goal

Access full-size printable charts using the QR code on page 192

Once you have completed your list (it may be pages and pages long!), take a look at the work you have completed and ensure you are not missing anything. We want to capture as much as we can, so we can create a blueprint from here. That said, everything is fluid—that is the beauty of this process—it moves and evolves as you grow and evolve.

As you review your goals, start to mark the ones that are categorically similar (often this is where you will start to see how some goals are interconnected—i.e., health, weight, working out . . .). I like to use a different color marker for each category, or sometimes I cut the list into strips and put them in piles. Once you have gone through this process, you will likely have a few big piles and a bunch of random piles or singles. For the moment, put the random/singles, though not unimportant, goals to the side.

Eat more organic vegetables

Open an investment account

Go to yoga 3x a week

Save for my retirement

Visit a naturopath

Do tax planning

Pla/

Go on a vacation

Hike the Grand Cany...

From here, really try to fine-tune the pile and try to get to the root of each goal. You may have more than one, but really try to reduce your list. One hundred goals, while awesome, can be overwhelming and can often lead to a lack of achievement.

You may start to see some patterns—very specifically on why a goal is important and how it fuels you.

Let me give you a personal example to further explain. I have always felt rather inadequate physically. My body and health state has never been a focus, and I've often felt either overweight or incapable of doing certain physical activities. And I've used a million excuses for not eating properly or exercising. After years of neglect, it has become a focus at this stage in my life. When I first recorded my goals there was a random list and these four were scattered among them. As I reviewed my list, I pulled these together because they were all connected.

Goal	Why this goal is important to me	How this goal fuels/inspires me
Eat Healthy	Healthier body, healthier mind, live longer able to do more	Achievement of this goal will enable me to live this next phase of my life easily without (or with minimal intended) health concerns.
Lose Weight	Overall confidence, clothes fit better	I have been at my ideal weight before and it made me feel great. I know that getting to a healthy weight will make me feel better overall. Also when I am at a particular weight, I am happier in my head!
Exercise Regularly	I don't love exercise, but I know it is important for me to maintain my mobility and do the things I want to do!	I know that by staying physically active I will be able to travel and do all the things I want to do in my life.
Scuba & Surf Regularly	I want to be able to scuba and surf easily—this requires both physical abilities and a lifestyle shift/ease. I love the freedom. I love the youthfulness. I love that I feel cool doing these things.	I love the water and being active and exploring. The water is like church for me. It fuels my body and soul. Plus I want to be a very cool grandparent and doing activities like these would give me cool creds!

Though written separately, you can see the correlation between the individual goals. It's important to understand each goal, why it is important, and how its achievement fuels you. This understanding helps you to become really connected to the goal and vastly increases your commitment to achieving it.

Goal	Why this goal is important to me	How this goal fuels/ inspires me

Access full-size printable charts using the QR code on page 192

Ideally, as you do this work, you will zone in on three to five priority goals that you are going to focus on. Many more than this and it can be a struggle to juggle daily responsibilities, legacy expectations, and achieving the milestone requirements (we are going to get to this) for each goal.

Remember, clarity breeds focus, and focus breeds mastery.

I trust with the example I provided you can see the connection among the goals and therefore a way to consolidate them and create one focused SMART goal.

What is a SMART goal you ask?

S = Specific—the goal is clear

M = Measurable—the goal is quantifiable

A = Achievable—it can happen with a plan

R = Relevant—it is the reason we do the work to understand the motivation of the goal

T = Time sensitive—there is a path with timelines for achieving the goal

Working with the example I provided, I can consolidate these health goals into one statement: *Over the course of the next X months, I will eat and exercise according to a regimented plan with the intent to work toward my goal of diving later this year and learning to surf, contingent on my travel plans next year.*

To further enhance this goal, it is ideal if you can add a multi-sensory and emotional reaction to the achievement goal. Rewrite the sentence as though you have achieved the goal.

I am so happy with my body and my fitness level. Eating healthy and exercising is now a normal part of my life, and I actually look forward to it. I am thrilled to be diving more regularly, and I love the feeling as I surf alongside my grandchildren. They think I am so cool and choose to spend time with me, which I truly love.

Now take this goal a couple of steps further—keeping in mind that the clearer we are, the more likely we will be to not only achieve our goal but to also achieve it sooner!

Goal: I am so happy with my body and my fitness level. Eating healthy and exercising is now a normal part of my life and I actually look forward to it. I am thrilled to be diving more regularly and I love the feeling as I surf alongside my grandchildren. They think I am so cool and choose to spend time with me which I truly love.

Is this goal what my heart truly desires?	What is my motivation to achieve this goal?	When do I plan to achieve this goal?	What tools (if any) do I need to make this happen?
Yes!	Overall health and well-being so I can live fully and be the coolest grandparent.	In xx, I plan to get to my ideal weight and fitness level and then maintain it from there.	Overall health assessment from my MD, fitness coach, and food coach.

Months Ahead	1	2	3	4	5	6
What are the key steps to make this happen?	MD assessment	Fitness coach, food coach, book learning	Regular workout (5x week) healthy eating	Ideal weight	Ongoing fitness regime	Scuba trip
Ideal timing (we will adjust as we map all goals together)	Mth/ xxxx	End of Mth/ xxx	D/M/YR	D/M/YR	Continuous	M/YR

The multisensory goal, accompanied by a picture of yourself in the center of the images that this goal conjures, will help to instill this goal in your consciousness. It will literally impact you every time you want to eat something unhealthy or make an excuse to not work out. Trust me—it works!

Work through the motivations, tools/support, and milestones that are required to achieve this goal. Leaning into my own health example, I do really want to be a grandmother who scuba dives and surfs. I have these images on my vision board and sentiments in my eulogy. Achievement of this goal is not something I decide today and it happens tomorrow, there are a series of things I need to put into place, and there are likely going to be some things that happen in life that challenge this plan—that's just life! Part of achieving my goal is getting to an ideal weight and an ideal fitness level, and then maintaining this so that when I am whatever age that I finally have these little people in my life, I will be able to achieve my goal. That said, there are some basic tools and things I need to do. In my case, I need to incorporate a fitness regime; I know that. I hate exercising and I struggle with managing my food intake, so I need a coach who helps to get and keep me on track and tells me what to do every day. I need this support and accountability. I am honest and up front about this and incorporate this into my plans. You will also see in the fleshing out of my plans that I am going to check in with my MD and review my supplements. I note the key milestones across the different months ahead.

In your case, there may be six months or sixty months—what matters is planning it out. Write out the steps and determine the appropriate timelines. This is a fundamental piece. If I pointed to a piece of land and said to somebody, go build a house, that's an overwhelming ask. But if you break down the steps, it's manageable, doable.

My ideal health state, active grandma example, is a goal that can be accomplished in the next year (maybe except for mastering surfing). Ultimately, I want to be a super cool grandparent—images of this are reflected in my vision board, and there are sentiments about being a cool grandma in my legacy/eulogy statement.

Using my example as a guideline, work through your top three to five goals. It is likely these goals have a one- to three-year horizon as we unconsciously tend to focus on key goals that we want to achieve sooner as opposed to later. However, as noted in my example, these goals often ladder up to other goals and your vision and your legacy/eulogy.

One of the last steps in this "goal clarification step" is to topline your goals onto one sheet so you can see how the timing works when you put them all together. I call this a Master Timeline. Upon reviewing what your total timeline for all your goals together looks like, you may want to make some timing adjustments.

It is important that you don't overcomplicate or over commit. Be realistic. You have a life and work right now—so plan out the achievement of your goals so you poise yourself for success. However, add as many time columns as you need and line up all of their goals and record the milestones. The point here is to see how the timing of all the goals line up. Done in isolation, the achievement of this individual goal may seem reasonable, but when you line up all your key three to five goals, you may need to adjust timing so that the plan is realistic with life. We want to set ourselves up for success here!

Goal:

MINI
VISION BOARD
REFLECTING
THE GOAL

Is this goal what my heart truly desires?	What is my motivation to achieve this goal?	When do I plan to achieve this goal?	What tools (if any) do I need to make this happen?

Months Ahead	1	2	3	4	5	6

Access full-size printable charts using the QR code on page 192

The truth is when we look at the goals in isolation we tend to think, *Yeah, in January I can do this, in February I can do this, and in March I can do this . . .* but when we put all the plans for all the top goals side by side, it may be too much. We may see there are ten things to be done in January, for example. That is now an unrealistic expectation. "Life is what happens while you're making other plans," and we are likely living a full and busy life now. We may need to make some adjustments to the timelines for each goal as we see it layered with the other goals. With the milestones for your three to five goals in front of you, make adjustments so that everything gets achieved. Reflect on this and spend some time here because I really want to ensure that after this exercise, you are happy with the top goals you have picked and you feel confident that you have created achievable timelines.

Master Timeline—tracks key milestones for your top three to five goals in one place.

Goals: Master Timeline of Key Milestones

Milestones	Month	Month	Month
Goal 1 & Date of Achievement			
Goal 2 & Date of Achievement			
Goal 3 & Date of Achievement			
Goal 4 & Date of Achievement			
Goal 5 & Date of Achievement			

** Identify the Milestone Markers that make the most sense for your goals: Months/Quarters/Years **

I love this part! Seeing the milestones and timelines all in one place makes me realize how achievable all my goals are! Call me crazy—and many do!—there is one more level of detail that helps make these goals a reality—it's the drill down! Before we get to the plotting out a plan and connecting all the dots, take a much-deserved break!

As you return from your break, ideally, lay key pages from the process out side by side so you can see them—or even better, post them up side by side on the wall so you can easily see them all at once. Seeing the pages all at once will allow you to start to ensure holistic alignment of everything—which is critical. If you can find a place where you can leave these key pages out while you ruminate and review, that would be awesome.

The key pages of which I am speaking are:

- Accomplishments

ACCOMPLISHMENTS List all of your accomplishments— big and small (size does not matter!)	How did this accomplishment make you feel?	What learning or benefit can you source from this accomplishment?

- Strengths

STRENGTHS List everything that makes you awesome. Ask yourself: What do I love about myself?	What are the ways that you could further optimize/leverage these strengths? (We often don't think about this!)

- Vision board

- Mission pages

Value	How YOU define this value	How this value shows up in your life. Provide an example.	Moving forward, how you will reflect this value in your life.

- Mission statement: My mission _____

- Values

What do I love to do?	What am I good at?	What can I be paid for?	What does the world need?
	Find your passion here	Find work that you enjoy and can get paid for here	Does the work you enjoy help others/ help the world?	

Can you see a connection?

- Legacy/eulogy statement

- Each of the five goal pages

Is this goal what my heart truly desires?	What is my motivation to achieve this goal?	When do I plan to achieve this goal?	What tools (if any) do I need to make this happen?
Yes!	Overall health and well-being so I can live fully and be the coolest grandparent.	In xx, I plan to get to my ideal weight and fitness level and then maintain it from there.	Overall health assessment from my MD, fitness coach, and food coach.

Months Ahead	1	2	3	4	5	6
What are the key steps to make this happen?	MD assessment	Fitness coach, food coach, book learning	Regular workout (5x week) healthy eating	Ideal weight	Ongoing fitness regime	Scuba trip
Ideal timing (we will adjust as we map all goals together)	Mth/ xxxx	End of Mth/ xxx	D/M/YR	D/M/YR	Continuous	M/YR

As you review all of these together, this is a good time to see what fits and what is not fitting. If everything feels as though it is consistent and coming together—great! However, if something feels out of place, then pull it aside and do some extra thinking here. We are going to go through this more in the next step. But I am planting the seed now for two reasons. First, note all the work that you have completed. This process is thorough; hence, the reason that I state that it is holistic—I truly have tried to bring together all the key aspects of our lives and all the different things that are mulling about in our heads. Second, it is in continuously surrounding ourselves in this material that we absorb it and the process. I want this to become part of your everyday life. I want the Life Blueprint process to be habitual/routine. **Akin to all the business management and planning processes and cycles that we so easily conduct in our business lives, ideally the Life Blueprint process will become second nature as a life-management tool.**

Live like your life depends on it because of course it does.

Step 7

Create a Game Plan—Plot a plan and connect all the dots

Before we move on to plotting and connecting all the dots, I want to talk about time and calendar management. It's okay if you rolled your eyes as you read that last sentence. Said no one ever, "Let's meet at the bar and chat about how we manage our calendar!" Managing priorities, meetings, activities, home, work, and life is challenging. And this becomes more complex when you add in a partner, kids, parents, grandparents, friends—we all get it. I have been on the search for a time-management system ever since I started working. I remember in my first month at work at Nestlé, a critical indoctrination and training of the new grad hires was taking "timetext." This system included a large three-ring binder with tabs for months, days, contacts, projects, and priorities. The two-day course (yup, two days) was intended to give us the tools we needed to manage. And I must admit, it did. We, and everyone else in the organization, carried our timetexts with us wherever we went, including holidays. It became our life-management system, and our "appropriate" use and mastery of it showed up in our performance reviews. This was back in the late '80s (I just rolled my eyes at myself for typing '80s—makes me feel old!), and while the system itself is archaic compared to the tools that we have today, many of the principles remain relevant.

149

I have evolved these principles and created a bit of a system for myself that I am going to share with you. It's not perfect and you will likely want to make some adaptations, but I can tell you it works. And I have the credibility to back it up. I have a boutique agency with several key clients and a healthy team that I comanage and co-inspire with other leaders; I coach and mentor (which I LOVE); I teach (also a passion) five or six unique courses at two different colleges to a new roster of students every three months; I have three rental properties, an Airbnb, and a home where I live, and I manage the properties, bills, and tenants for all of these; I have three adult children, two of whom live in different time zones and are a minimum of an eight-hour plane ride away; I have a healthy, though aging, mom whom I check in on daily; and I have my own health and well-being and that of my trusted companion Sadie, who goes with me everywhere. My car is stocked with critical hand tools, a drill, chain saw, shovel, salt, a change of clothes, protein bars, water, dog food and treats, and a blanket at all times. I run events, host gatherings, and do all the things. I am not sharing any of this to brag. Truthfully, most people judge and tell me I'm crazy. It's true, but everything I do, I do because I actually love it! I wake up happy and go to bed exhausted but fulfilled. My life is far from perfect, but it is full, so I have calendar management down to a freaking science. But as you will see, it is not scientific at all.

While there are a myriad of tools out there, I keep it pretty basic.

I have two critical tools:

- An online calendar—I use Windows, but if you use iCal or Google, it makes no difference. The objective here is to have a place where you can book meetings for work and also schedule personal/life appointments.

- An old school calendar at-a-glance book. I especially love it when I find one that is light and can double as a work notebook. But often these can get clunky, so I have a notebook for work notes and tasks and my calendar at-a-glance book. Often these books have year-at-a-glance pages for the year you are in and the one ahead, which is ideal. If you can't find these, print them off and/or check my website, as I offer one online.

Now let me share how I manage my goals, my work, my life—all the things.

Let's go back to your goals and start to pull everything together and connect all the dots. Remember the chart Goals: Master Timeline of Key Milestones; print this out or have it at your fingertips. With your critical tools in front of you (your online calendar and a hard copy of month-at-a-glance and the years-at-a-glance—the year you are in and the year ahead), you are ready to seize the days!

In order of priority, put all of these events in your online calendar. Go as far into the future as you possibly can.

1. Work meetings

    - The weekly, the monthly, the quarterly, the annual. What you don't know for sure, still mark with a hold. This will ensure you check in as the date gets closer, and the good news is that you will have reserved time.
    - Ensure that as you move forward, all meeting invites and calendar notices are recorded in your calendar.

2. Holidays

    - Record any statutory holidays, and if you have kids, all the days when they don't have school or when they have scheduled holidays.
    - Mark the days and weeks you personally want to take off.

3. Celebrations, annual events, etc.

    - Birthdays, religious holidays, etc. Mark them all in.

4. Personal health and wellness. Now that you have all "the things" for which you are "responsible" and often accountable to others, it's time to put in your stuff!

    - MD, dentist, therapy appointments—put them all in.
    - Gym and exercise schedule.
    - I block off 5–7 a.m. every morning for my personal time. I work with people in a multitude of different time zones, and as such I ensure I block off my personal time. People book time with me by either sending me an invite (which I can accept, decline, or propose a new time) or through an app such as Calendly, which only allows bookings according to the availability I have provided.

5. Legacy matters. Remember that legacy exercise. Remember the things you noted in how you want to be remembered, "the breaths you want to take away." For the relationships and things that are separate from your goals, look at your calendar and see where and when you would like to book time to do these things that really matter. For example, the monthly family Sunday lunch, the weekly lunch with your mom, the x number of times per year you are going to volunteer at a soup kitchen or shelter . . . book those things in. Some of these may start to connect to your goals, which is great; mark them in.

The goal of your "online" calendar is to ensure blocks of time are continuously noted and updated. It is your "nitty gritty" "in the weeds" time-management system. I put everything in mine, even reminders for key bill payments to ensure money is in the right places (due to my rental properties).

The objective of your month- and year-at-a-glance calendar is to provide the view from the proverbial "50,000 feet." And this is where we are going to start to connect the dots between your goals and your present-day life (as reflected in your online calendar).

Bring this completed chart forward.

Milestones	Month	Month	Month
Goal 1 & Date of Achievement			
Goal 2 & Date of Achievement			
Goal 3 & Date of Achievement			
Goal 4 & Date of Achievement			
Goal 5 & Date of Achievement			

** Identify the Milestone Markers that make the most sense for your goals: Months/Quarters/Years **

Mark in your calendar the key month- and year-at-a-glance milestones that you noted. You are welcome to use a template like the ones provided if they help you get even more organized before you input into your calendar at a glance. I provide all the different formats because everyone has different methods for tracking and planning. Use what works for you. The objective is to get critical milestone deadlines into your calendar at a glance.

Goals: _____ (year)

Goal	Jan	Feb	March	April	May	June
Goal 1						
Goal 2						
Goal 3						
Goal 4						
Goal 5						

··

Access full-size printable charts using the QR code on page 192

··

Write what you identified needed to be completed by a certain date into the corresponding calendar at a glance (month and/or year). Because this is so important. Because this is where the rubber meets the road, I am bringing forward my example.

Remember I shared my "surfing/diving cool grandma goal" and it had its own series of timelines. And I asked you to do this for your top five goals. Then I asked you to take the bottom row from your top five goal charts and input into your master timeline of key milestones so we could apply a "stress test." While each individual goal likely has its own cadence and rhythm, it is critical to the achievement of each individual and then the cumulative goals that the timelines also be looked at together. The intent is to see if your plans, when compiled together, are achievable or if you need to make any adjustments. Optimizing timing optimizes the plan and ensures completion of all timelines, which ladders up to the achievement of goals! **Baby steps lead to leaps of achievement!**

MINI
VISION BOARD
REFLECTING
THE GOAL

Is this goal what my heart truly desires?	What is my motivation to achieve this goal?	When do I plan to achieve this goal?	What tools (if any) do I need to make this happen?		

Months Ahead	1	2	3	4	5	6

Milestones	Month	Month	Month
Goal 1 & Date of Achievement			
Goal 2 & Date of Achievement			
Goal 3 & Date of Achievement			
Goal 4 & Date of Achievement			
Goal 5 & Date of Achievement			

** Identify the Milestone Markers that make the most sense for your goals:
Months/Quarters/Years **

Somewhere on each of the month-at-a-glance pages, record the milestones that need to be accomplished for that month. Do the same for the year-at-a-glance. This month, this week, and tomorrow. The last phase in this is to carry forward your plans into the days and weeks ahead. I like to do some of this in my digital calendar and some in a paper calendar. My digital calendars show blocks of booked time: meetings, appointments, workouts, dinner events, family events, celebrations, and even my morning routine (me time). I also block off time, as though it is a meeting, when I work on the activities required for the achievement of my goals. For example, I blocked off time to write this book. This would show up in a time slot in my digital calendar as "Book Writing."

In my month-/year-at-a-glance calendars, I record key calls and follow-ups that I need to make happen but do not necessarily require a time block. I will certainly make time for them, but I might do them during my lunch break or while I am driving (hop on a conference call). The things that I record in my written calendar are more like a to-do list.

This is very subjective and works for me. Do what works for you. The key is to ensure that whatever method you choose, you stay on track and adjust as required.

I will tell you now that working through your goals is the most arduous part of the process because you really have to think through the steps and timelines and lay them all out. I can also tell you that once you do this, it is a huge relief because now you just follow the plan. We often work in this level of detail at work. Yet in our personal lives, we do not. Why is that? Because we are paid? Because we will get fired if we do not? Because we need to provide a pathway to success for the brands and services and companies we work for? Remember, our lives are the most valuable thing we have—there is no more worthy use of your time than to create a life plan!

After you have completed planning all your time, you may be wondering what to do with all the other goals that you listed. They still matter, they just didn't make it into the "Top 5," but their day may come. As you achieve your other goals, these ones may move up the ladder.

Take the time now to list them and identify why they matter and the intended year of achievement. This template will hopefully now exist for you in perpetuity, allowing you to continuously add to the list as you evolve through life. And as a goal makes it into the Top 5, repeat the calendar management process we just did. Ideally, this entire process will become second nature to you.

Goal	Why this goal is important to me	How this goal fuels/ inspires me	Ideal date of achievement

Access full-size printable charts using the QR code on page 192

I know this exercise can feel onerous, but once it's done, it's done and you just update as you go along. Calendar management has been critical to balancing my vision with my day-to-day work and accountabilities with my intended legacy. Calendar management is critical to balancing life—the present and the future. It is critical to your life!

> *A dream is a dream until there is a date and a plan to achieve it.*

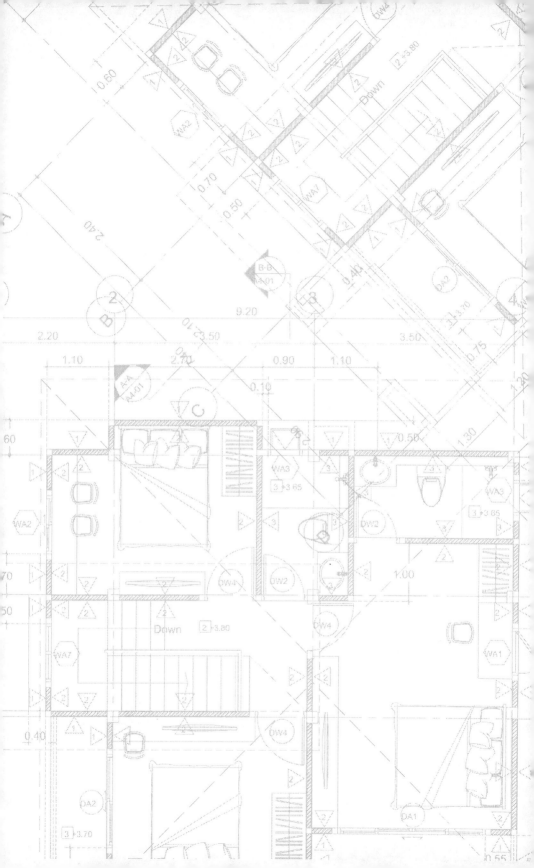

Step 8

Gut Check—Holistic alignment of the Total Blueprint for your life

Head, heart, and gut—if these are not in sync, then we are out of sync. Now is the time to ensure all the work you have done up to this point is in sync. There was a method to my madness when I asked you to take pauses, go for walks, tape things to the wall, or lay all your work out so you could see it. My intent was for you to constantly reflect, ruminate, reorganize, add, and delete. If you have not done that, do that now. In fact, if you haven't done it, then I would like you to try something you may not have done before. I would like you to do a review tomorrow! I am going to ask you to review everything very consciously (I provide more detail soon) and then go to bed and sleep on it. When you get up in the morning, do a review. I cannot stress enough how important it is that you feel good about everything and how it has come together. That you feel good in your head, your heart, and your gut! Research has proven that when we review something or evaluate a problem before we go to bed, our mind will continue to work on it while we sleep. So consciously review and then go to bed!

Okay, so this is what I mean by a conscious review before you go to sleep. Let's grab a coffee (or whatever suits your fancy) and backtrack to review! In groundwork Step 2, we worked through fears, distraction, derailers, limiting beliefs, and challenges. While there may still be work to do to manage some of these issues, what we did commit to was that they would not hold us back. Our momentum is moving us forward.

Do you feel like you have poised yourself to move forward positively? If not, take the time to deal with any of these issues. Go back and reread Step 2. Even be so bold as to follow the ritual that I suggested and burn everything (safely). This ritual will remind you that you cannot change the past or these issues. You can learn from them. You can work on healing. And very importantly, you can choose to move forward.

You then identified your Accomplishments and Strengths—these are ideally taped to the wall or still laid out on the table in front of you.

Vision—look at your amazing vision board! I hope it makes you smile, feel joy, and inspires you. Ensure you put it somewhere that you can see it several times a day and very specifically when you wake up and before you go to sleep.

Your Mission/Purpose work, Your Eulogy, and Your Values. Review all of these also.

And last, your goals with the drill downs, the parameter exercise for the next year, and your key factors for success.

With everything in front of you either on the wall or on the table, do a conscious and methodical review.

Does everything feel as though it is aligned? Do you feel as though you have a holistic plan? How do your head, heart, and gut feel? Now go to bed and meet me back here in the morning!

So, how are you feeling after a good night's sleep? Is there anything that needs tweaking? If yes, make the adjustments now and review again. This part of the process is important because this is where everything comes together and you feel as though you have a clear, solid, achievable plan that is holistically integrated.

As a final "litmus test," let's take stock. Do you remember in one of the first steps of the Life Blueprint process we did a "Taking Stock" exercise and I told you we would come back to it? Well, here it is!

With all the work you have done in front of you, on your table or on the wall, as a reference, complete the following chart. For the year ahead, prioritize your areas of focus, then establish the grade that you intend to achieve. Spending time on these key parameters now, with all of your other work in front of you, will ensure everything is in alignment. I cannot stress enough how important alignment is. When we are aligned, everything flows!

Parameter	Health	Partner/ Relation- ship	Family, Children, Parents, Siblings	Friends, Social Life	Job/ Career	Money	Religion/ Spirituality	Volunteer/ Impact/ Charitable Work
Priority 1-8 1= Top priority 8= Least priority								
Assess how you think you are doing A=All good B= Could be better C= Area for development								

Access full-size printable charts using the QR code on page 192

In completing this, you will have closed the loop on the process. You are done . . . for the moment. **You have created the blueprint for your life. You have "built castles in the sky" and foundations to ground them and ensure sustenance. And because you have completed the entire process, you now only need to iterate and update as you move through life. This process will serve you for life, and I hope you use it that way.**

Use it to check in weekly, monthly, quarterly, and annually to review and access how things are going. We trust these processes for business, and they work. Trust this process for your life—I guarantee it works!

This step was one of the fundamental reasons I created the Life Blueprint process. (I am laughing at myself as I type that line—how many times have you read it up to this point? Truth is, I created the Life Blueprint process for a multitude of reasons, and each step has been consciously crafted, everything is critical and fundamental.) Everything I had read, all the courses I had taken, all provided one of the steps you have worked through, but there was nothing that brought all the steps together in one place. In business, we author a business plan. Business plans are cohesive, all-encompassing, visionary, and time sensitive. Yet in life we don't have a similar process. Scratch that, we haven't had a similar process until now!

The Life Blueprint process is cohesive, integrated, and holistic. It connects all the pieces of our human life. You build/design it step-by-step so that everything fits, like the pieces of a puzzle. This helps you to stay inspired, on track, and make your dreams a reality.

Welcome to the house of your design leveraging the Life Blueprint process. Welcome to your Life House—it will be your lighthouse as you journey forward.

VISION:				
Mission/Purpose:				
Goal:	Goal:	Goal:	Goal:	Goal:
Plans & timing to achieve each goal:				
Values:				
Key Factor for Success:				

Access full-size printable charts using the QR code on page 192

Welcome to your
EXTRAORDINARY LIFE!

Step 9

Shit Will Happen—
Continuous evolution, iteration, or pivot

There are days when lying in bed, watching TV, and doing nothing is all our mind and body can muster. Give yourself these days—without judgment, without remorse. We need to refuel. We need to "do nothing." We need to rest in order to regenerate. And then, after we rest, we need to get back to "the work." Add to this that there are going to be some unexpected surprises and twists and turns in your journey. You are going to fall in love. You are going to fall out of love. You are going to get promoted or start a new job or get a transfer. You may lose your job and decide to pursue a new career or perhaps travel the world! Bottom line, whether we like it or not, things will happen.

When things happen, we can choose how we want to deal with them. **The most amazing thing about the Life Blueprint process is that when something expected or unexpected happens, you have a methodical plan in front of you and you can consciously choose how you want to navigate the challenge/opportunity**. Because you have done the work, it is easier to figure out if you want to **stay the course, evolve, iterate, or pivot** and do a complete overhaul—the choice is yours. Let's break these down a little further.

Stay the course

When opportunities or challenges arise, you may opt to keep doing what you are currently doing. There may be a greater plan or need at stake. That is okay! I often think that when there is an opportunity or issue, we feel as though we need to change. We don't. We can stay on the course that we have planned for ourselves. Evaluate and make the conscious choice . . . that is the key!

Evolve

Often as we put the Life Blueprint into practice, two things happen:

We start to achieve our goals much more quickly. Where we had initially forecasted that it was going to take three years to achieve a goal, we achieve it in one year. This happens more often than not. And it happens because we laid out a plan, and in doing so, we mapped out all the steps, so we naturally move through them much more easily than we expected. We flow! As a result, we start to build on the goals achieved and add more goals evolving the entire Life Blueprint process.

We realize a few months after completing the Life Blueprint process that we have had some revelations. We were working toward a plan, but we gained so much learning through the process and putting it into place that we want to make some changes. The growth has enhanced our awareness of who we are and our purpose, and as such we now have a bolder plan stirring within us which leads to iterate or pivot.

Iterate

By definition, to iterate means to modify, enhance, nuance . . . until it feels right. When applied to the Life Blueprint process, it means to massage our plan until it feels holistic and aligned. As we start to put everything into place, we may want or need to make some adjustments—there is nothing wrong with that. In fact, that is why it is a blueprint—because we can modify it as we go along!

I usually do this on Sunday mornings. I do a check-in on how I am tracking on getting things accomplished, what's working, what's not, and I make adjustments. The beautiful thing about this is that I am simply adjusting a plan that is in place, I am not starting at ground zero, nor am I scratching my head wondering what to do. All the principles and tools that guide me are right in front of me.

Pivot

Sometimes we do start all over again. I have seen this happen a couple of times. In these cases, it is usually for one of two reasons. The first is that the person was not truly clear and honest with themselves as they went through the process. You need to be selfish as you work through the Life Blueprint process. In Step 1, when we dream BIG, sometimes people hold back. Don't hold back! In Step 2, when we work through our fears, distractions, derailers, limiting beliefs, and challenges, we do this so that we can put these in their place and not have them interfere as we move forward. The work we do in the second step is very important in clearing out clutter and/or baggage so that we can move on. When we don't take that time, it is as though a cloud casts a shadow over all the other plans we create.

The second reason we pivot is because there may have been a life-altering occurrence—this can be like winning the lottery or facing a huge trauma or health issue. An extreme situation may cause us to do a rewrite of the entire plan or parts of it. On a positive note, you now have the formula and having gone through the process once makes going through it a second (or more) time easier.

Evolving, iterating, and pivoting do not encompass every little thing that could happen. Let's be honest, there are going to be days when your head is not in the game. There are going to be days when you lose track, when you get caught up in life. There could even be weeks. You will know you have fallen off track—there will be some legitimate reasons and there will be some excuses—the key is to get back on track. Don't dwell. Don't beat yourself up. Just get back to it.

I have fallen off track. I have strayed. It happens. Over time, though, I have created a series of rituals and routines that are so connected to my physical and mental health and well-being that I only fall off track for maybe one or two days, if at all anymore. These routines/rituals/practices—call them whatever suits your fancy—are so critical that I refer to them as "Key Factors for Success." We use this expression in business to define critical business requirements that must remain in place in order for business to keep operating in spite of all other issues/conditions. As a human, we have basic needs such as food, water, and sleep that are critical requirements for our survival. However, there are often other requirements that ensure we are motivated and inspired with a healthy mind, body, and spirit. These are our human key factors for success (KFS).

For every person, these KFS are unique. In my case, I will share a few that help me stay on track and motivated.

1. Morning routine:

For me, mornings are my favorite time of day. I love getting an early start, and I very naturally wake up most days between 5–5:30 a.m. (I go to bed pretty early). When I wake up, the first thing I see is my vision board and my key goals. They are literally on the wall in front of me. I look at them and remind myself to get out of bed and stay the course. I affirm that today will be a great day.

I get out of bed, head to the bathroom, brush my teeth, etc. I then have a lemon water with ginger, turmeric, and cayenne, and either do a meditation inside the house or do a walking meditation with my dog, Sadie.

I come back, take my vitamins, and exercise. I hate exercising, so if I don't do it first thing, I won't do it. I know this about myself. My point in sharing is to know yourself. Know the things you struggle with and get them done and out of the way. Eventually, doing them will become habitual and the hate will lessen or go away. Admittedly, I have found an exercise regime that I like, so I follow it a minimum of five out of seven days. It is a maximum of twenty minutes, but it stretches me and keeps me flexible and healthy—and able to achieve one of my key goals.

With my exercise complete, I put on coffee, then shower. I try to fast until noon, but sometimes (okay, most times) I have a scoop of almond butter with my coffee. I love it!

Music plays continuously in the background. I love Spotify. Depending on my mood, I will ask Alexa to put on a "happy vibes" playlist or a "dance mix" or "happy country"—did you know that country music is actually good for our brain health? It's true! Check out Doc Amen in the back of this book (Suggested reading and other things of interest). And I may read for ten to twenty minutes, then journal. (FYI, I post daily journal prompts on IG because so many have asked for support in this area. If you need any support here, check out my IG Nicole_gallucci)

At around 7:00 a.m., I begin my workday.

Now there are some days when I am up and out of the house by 5:30 a.m., so I skip or move some of these things until later in the day. Sadie and I still walk, and I meditate in stride. I usually skip my workout, take what's left of my lemon water and my coffee to go, and crank the tunes in the car until I settle into an audiobook or podcast.

My point is that I still keep parts of the routine going.

2. Evening routine:

My evening routine is even more critical on the nights preceding a 5:30 a.m. departure!

Regardless, I prepare my lemon et. al water for the next day and make a soothing tea to take to bed.

I prep my clothes, plan my meals, and anything else for the next day, then I hop into bed.

I often work in bed before I actually go to sleep—usually this starts around 8 p.m. I will finish off anything urgent and review what I need to do the following day(s). I always try to be one to two days ahead of daily work, otherwise I am stressed. In addition, things often "come up," so being ahead allows me to juggle. With my work done, I read, write, do a legacy check-in (Did I live and act today the way I want to be remembered? What can I learn/do tomorrow?), watch a doc or YouTube video, and chill.

Sometime around 9:00 p.m., I shut down. With my eyes closed, I say my own version of prayers and gratitudes, and I bless my children. And I tell Sadie, my ever-faithful companion, that I love her, I give her one last scratch on the head, and I fall asleep.

3. Friday morning work management:

I am typically only available for a few hours on Fridays; they are critical personal workdays. I book myself off until 10 a.m. to review the past week and what needs to get done for the following week. Then amid getting work done such as paying bills, working on client documents, and connecting with the team, I try to avoid any external meetings. I also use this time to prep my home for the weekend. I like everything to be fresh and clean for the weekend so I can feel as though I can take a break.

I made this change to my Friday routine because I found that between the volume of chores and errands that needed to get done on Saturday and the scaries that ensued at some point on Sunday, I had either been too busy or had fretted away my weekend. I found that if I actually spent some time on Friday mornings prepping for the week ahead, I could let the work worry go and really enjoy my weekends.

I also use my Fridays to review calendar meetings and plans for the upcoming weeks. It's not just about making sure all my upcoming meetings are booked but also that I've scheduled lunches and breaks needed for my personal health and well-being, as well as ensuring that any of my extracurricular activities (i.e., hockey games, yoga workouts, etc.) are in my calendar. I really do mark all these things weeks in advance. We plan work meetings two or three weeks in advance, why not life meetings?! I find if I book in all my personal activities, I stick to them. Sure there may be adjustments, but the point is that they are in fact simply adjustments. Timing is adjusted versus eliminating or forgetting about key activities. I found that when I didn't do this planning, I would get frustrated and resentful because I would have missed doing the things that were important to me because I allowed other events and/ or activities to fill up my calendar. By doing this planning, I manage with conscious intent, and should I choose to modify or cancel something, I do so fully aware of the implications.

Managing my Friday mornings as I have shared has been a BIG game changer for me. This planning has released so much stress and anxiety and made my weekends so much nicer.

4. Sunday morning personal management:

I LOVE Saturday and Sunday mornings. But there is something sacred about Sundays. Perhaps it is because in many belief systems, it is a day of rest, a day for religion, a day for family. For me, it is a time to review, refresh, and plan (but differently than on Fridays). My Sunday mornings are peaceful, they are a gift, and they are mine. Sundays are kind of sacred. I like to get up before everybody else in the house is up and really have some quiet time. My writing seems to flow on Sundays. In addition, this is when I work on my own personal goals and personal projects. Sundays are one of the critical goal check-in points that I have referred to on several occasions. I review the past week and then look forward at the weeks, months, and years ahead (hence, the month- and year-at-a-glance I mentioned in Step 7). I review how I am tracking against the milestones I set and decide if I need to make any adjustments. Leaning into a business analogy, this is my weekly check-in with my boss (me). I find that this check-in becomes very routine, akin to the Friday morning work review. Again, this rigor sets me up for success. On Monday mornings there isn't the need or desire to pull the blanket over my head and escape the world. Rather, I can start the week with a degree of ease and direction, which is very confidence building and peaceful.

For those of you with partners, families, or others who influence your calendar, I suggest a Sunday check-in using the week- and month-at-a-glance formats. Post it in a visible place in your living space, as I find that this tool really helps to keep everyone informed and on track. You can see each other's activities and manage together ahead of time versus having chaotic and stressful time management. Let's be honest: as soon as we are responsible or connected to others, we need to take their requirements into consideration—this is so much easier when there is transparency and planning! Cocreating plans can save everyone's sanity. As a single, self-employed mom, I have experience here, so trust me on this one. And I really do think it needs to be visible and posted on a wall that everyone can see. I tried the online version—it doesn't work. There is always something that gets missed. With the one on the wall in a visible, high-traffic place, updates are easy as are conversations around adjustments, pickups, drop-offs, future plans—it is all right in front of you.

Last, I do a legacy check-in. Do I need to add any plans to my week to ensure I am "living my legacy" every day?

5. A muse:

Historically, a muse has been a person—often a woman—who is a source of artistic inspiration. Obviously, that is not what I am talking about. We all need a muse—the modern-day definition! A muse today is a source of inspiration, whatever moves you and inspires you into action. And ideally a situation or something that you can control (versus a person). It could be an amazing cup of coffee where you savor the heat, the taste, the moment. It could be sitting on a park bench gazing at a pond or watching children laughing in a playground without a care in the world. What I am suggesting is that you identify something that helps you to be creative, adventurous, and resilient.

I have a few different muses. My first is bookstores. I LOVE bookstores—specifically private ones that have a blend of old and new books and ideally someone older with spectacles behind the counter. You know the ones—they look grumpy, but truthfully they are a bastion of information and don't suffer fools—these are my people.

My next muse is nature. A swim, a paddle, a walk in nature (ideally with Sadie) will sometimes be exactly what the doctor ordered! Nature truly is the ultimate medicine. I will frequently ground and/or hug a tree and/or forage for flowers. Galleries and museums are also great muses. I am not the stereotypical gallery/museum guest. I move through at a pretty steady pace and when something catches my eye, it is the story beside the work that usually captivates me. I am a sucker for a good story!

I've shared various options because I work all over, and as such, I use different places and spaces to inspire me. I use these spaces as a catalyst for ideas, to get me out of a funk, or as places to restore my energy. Sometimes these options are not easy, and that is when I turn toward a few very simple go-tos. These are really daily habits for me. I burn sage and/or incense and meditate every morning, but if at any point in the day I need a quick refresh, I take a few minutes and I light a candle, burn some incense, and listen to a meditation. The ritual alone calms me, and if I add some gentle music and a fresh cup of tea or coffee, well, then I am quickly calmed, transformed, and ready to be productive again.

My point in sharing all of this is that you can't expect to be delivering and inspiring 100 percent of the time. You need to refuel, and to do that you need to give yourself access or stimuli that will induce creativity and inspiration.

My tools:

I am a knapsack person. My motto is "have knapsack will travel." My knapsack contains everything I need to be functional anywhere.

- Mobile phone—obviously.
- Laptop—with all my files on it, so I can do anything, anywhere.
- External hard drive—because heaven forbid something happens to my laptop, I have a backup. Yes, I back up to the cloud and I use online services, but sometimes you need an external hard drive (according to all my IT friends!).
- iPad—because although I love books, I travel often and am trying to love digital reading. This is a work in progress, and admittedly, I like the iPad for this the best. I also use it for creative projects.
- Journal(s)—my personal journal for capturing notes and ideas and my business journal for work thoughts and follow-ups.
- Incense and sage (sometimes a candle)—I burn incense daily and sage as required. I find them soothing. They clear negative energy and make mine more positive and focused!
- Cue cards—I have cards for each client and key passwords/apps that require account information and further details. I also use them for coaching prompts and exercises at workshops. And I use them to capture ideas.
- Sticky notes and a black marker. If you follow me on IG, then you know I frequently post a pic with a sticky note on my forehead that identifies a "Note to self" sharing a learning that I think might also resonate with others.

- Markers, a small set of paints, watercolor paper, glue stick, tape, and small scissors—because sometimes I want to be creative visually, so I always have supplies with me.

6. Music:

There is always music playing when I work or play. I love all kinds of music and curate what I need for the mood I am in.

I have shared transparently here to give you a sense of what my KFS are and the role they play in my life. Take the time to figure out what these are for you. Make a list and get what you need. Shit can happen when you least expect it. And often when it does happen, we default to habits, rituals, and routines because they give us security and comfort. Now is your opportunity to consciously define what those practices and tools are. With repeated use, they will become habitual. They will become your key factors for success. They will keep you stable when the ground beneath you feels as though it is shifting. So, set yourself up for success and identify some practices and tools that ensure you are always good to go!

Key Factors For Success

Key Factor	Why it matters	What do you need to ensure you make this key factor happen (tools, time, focus ...)

Access full-size printable charts using the QR code on page 192

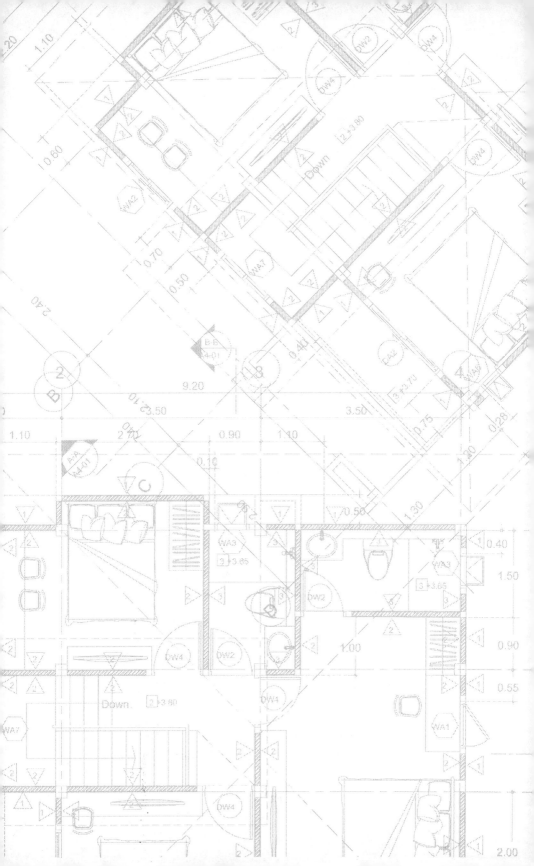

Step 10

Live Your Best Life—It's yours in the making!

For all intents and purposes, you are done. Your home is complete—for the moment. There is a roof over your head, which points skyward daily inspiring you to work toward your vision. A firm foundation of values rooted in footings of key factors for success will hold you safe when the ground quakes. And in between the roof and the floor lies beams that brace the structure and ensure its stability—these are your mission and legacy; and the rooms within are your goals—always in motion as you achieve the milestones that complete them and then go on to develop new ones or raise the bar higher.

To be fair and 100 percent honest, your home will never be complete. It—like you—is a work in progress. Life is a work in progress. What you have done by completing the Life Blueprint process is put an important stake in the ground. You have created a blueprint for your life by design and desire. You have worked through each of the steps and reflected along the way. As such, you have created a plan that is holistically interconnected—it feels good and feels achievable. It all makes sense with who you are and what you stand for. As a result, it will flow. You may find it hard to believe that it will flow, but it will. I am proof, as are thousands of others who have gone through the process. Sure, there will be struggles, but you are now armed with all the tools you need to either accept the challenge or navigate around it. Every life decision you will make now as you move forward will be consistent with the plan you have created. And if there is an inconsistency, you will know. The feeling of flow will stop. There will be a niggling feeling in your stomach. You will know something is off. Take the time to reflect, then course correct or adjust, and move on.

Embrace the future with open and excited arms! From here, you will grow, change, and face new opportunities and challenges. These may cause you to reflect on your blueprint and perhaps even consider making changes. The good news is that any changes will be from a place of conscious and deliberate intent! Life and therefore the Life Blueprint process is an ever-growing, ever-evolving process. The GREAT NEWS is that you have a tool that will serve you for life. Because you have a plan, you can alter it decisively. **Isn't your life worth conscious deliberate intent and decisiveness?!**

Hell yes!

Sound the drumroll as you look at the blueprint you have created for the steps and stages in front of you.

As I shared throughout the book, my life did not go as I initially planned. And I sense the same may have been true for you or you likely would not be holding this book in your hand. I didn't want to miss out on the potential and fullness of life. I needed a solve. Once I "woke up" and had the awareness that I needed to really work through a plan for my life with the same, if not greater, diligence that I put into raising my children or doing my job, I created the Life Blueprint process. And since creating it, I have not looked back. The Life Blueprint process helped me to make conscious life choices that are in sync with who I am and what I stand for. When I have been lost or confused, the process has helped me to refocus and ground myself. The diligence and consciousness of the process have always been my guiding light. This guiding light has become my vocation. I am on a mission to share this process with as many people as possible.

I opened this book with perspective-stimulating learnings from Viktor Frankl on the meaning of life—sharing the Life Blueprint process has become critical to my meaning. But it has also added to the sweetness of my own life. Let me explain by closing with learnings from Paulo Coelho. Coelho is best known for his book *The Alchemist*. In the book, he refers to the quest to find the "Elixir of life." Throughout the novel, the main character, Santiago, learns that the true elixir of life lies in recognizing the interconnectedness of all things, understanding the language of the Universe, and very importantly, **finding fulfillment in the pursuit of dreams**. It is a metaphor for living a purposeful life, being in harmony with oneself and the world, and embracing the journey of self-realization and spiritual growth.

It is my hope in defining and serving up to the world the Life Blueprint process that I have provided the tool to unlock our inner alchemist and realize that we are both the elixir and the seeker of ingredients to stimulate it to its full potential.

In my opinion, that elixir is unique to each and every one of us. I do not profess to be anything more a than human in search of my elixir. I have found it, the elixir, in the many magical and important relationships in my life and in the angst, challenges, and trauma of life that forced me to find a strength and a will to live inside myself that some days was elusive. I have found it in blessed homes and spaces, especially our cottage, that while extremely humble, has provided immeasurable safety, security, and peace. And I have found the spice to my elixir in the work I have been privileged to do and the world I have been privileged to explore through travel. Please notice that not all my elixirs have been sweet and savory. In fact, some have been bitter and life threatening, but it is in living and learning through both that we create a life worth living and sharing. Today, my proverbial container of elixir is overflowing in fulfillment but far from complete. And my hope is that I unlock for everyone the freedom and faith to figure out and pursue their own elixir.

As I type, I have shared the Life Blueprint process with thousands of people. My goal is to share it with the world. Though I am oversimplifying the point, just as a nail needs a hammer, I think life needs a guide. In the process of living life and creating this guide, I have learned a few other things along the way that I want to share while I have you captive!

1. The (most) clichés are timeless and true. They are the quotes we continuously read and the ones that start chapters in books. They are the sentiments shared at celebrations in life and of death. They are timeless words of wisdom.

2. What is meant to be will be. There are energies and truths beyond our wildest dreams, and these guide us and teach us every single day.

3. Stay the course. If you have a plan and you have created this plan with deliberate, conscious intent, stay, don't stray. There will be many temptations to stray, but these are only in your path to test your faith in yourself and your commitment. Staying takes much more fortitude than straying.

4. Do no harm. I trust this requires no explanation?! We will cause harm. It is inevitable. The intent is that we do not do deliberate harm.

5. Our humanity is universal. We are far from alone, though we often think we are alone. Everyone worries. Everyone hurts. Everyone loves. Everyone wants. Everyone needs. You get it. There are others everywhere. You are not alone.

6. Leave a legacy you are proud of. Own your successes as much as your failures, and share so others can learn, and you can hopefully make their lives easier. Live and die with as few, if any, regrets as possible.

7. Love with all you've got, and share your love generously. Love is the ultimate elixir. It can kill and it can cure—use it to cure. I firmly believe love can cure all things.

8. Rules were made to be broken. Who made the rules? When were they made? Do they make sense? I am a disruptor, but in the context of all the points made so far. If a rule doesn't feel right in your gut, listen to your gut.

9. Life is what happens while you are making other plans. Treasure the moments you are in because they quickly become our past, unchangeable, and if we are not cautious, forgotten and undervalued.

10. Forgive. Forgive yourself. Forgive others. There is no victory in holding a grudge or harboring hate. There are few things I know for sure. But one thing I do know is that we all have imperfections, and sometimes these inadvertently hurt others. (This is a topic I'll explore in a future book.) Please forgive us our foibles.

11. (Why eleven points? Eleven is my number—it shows up for me every single day without fail!) Begin with the end—remind yourself every morning to live your day fully and think about what that will look like at the end of the day, the week, the month, the year, your life.

This book and the global sharing of the Life Blueprint is my "end." I am on a mission because it is my mission to share the Life Blueprint process with as many people as possible in the hopes of helping them create full lives. I hope that it has helped you. If you are reading these words, then I know it has. AMEN! And assuming that is the case and it impacted you, I would ask you to pay it forward. To gift this book to someone, leave it on a park bench, the seat on a bus, or in the pocket of an airplane. Leave a note in it so that the next reader knows it was not lost but rather placed there to be found. If together we have had the opportunity to support even one person on their quest for more and/or better, then we have achieved the goal of impact, "of taking away a breath," and of making the world a better place. And take a pic and send it to me or post it and tag me. Please read to "The End" and stay connected with me. Share your story. Post your pics, write letters, join me online and off. Share your evolution, your victories, and the learnings from your challenges. Share your "castles in the air" and the foundations that you built under them. **It is from our cumulative learning and sharing that we can provide wisdom and ideally pave an easier path for future generations**. And if nothing else, we can foster hope. I do believe it springs eternal.

Now, go live! Find love in the life you have today and follow your blueprint so that you continue to nurture the love.

With you all the way and wishing you EXTRAORDINARY!

Nicole

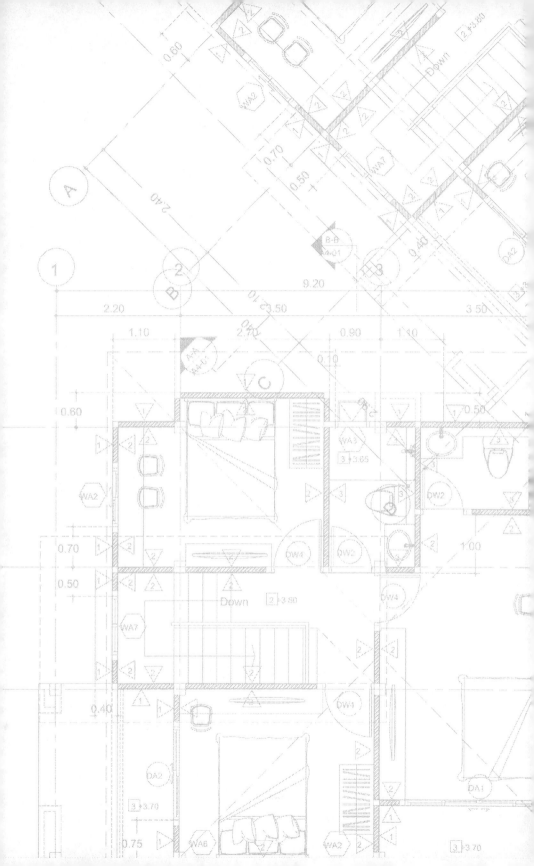

The End

Actually, this is a never-ending story. Isn't that the magic of life? That it is cyclical and never ending? What does that mean for us? In writing this book, I have put an important stake in the ground for myself and for the Life Blueprint process—technically, this is like a day one! But the truth is, I continuously speak globally about the Life Blueprint process, I run workshops, I offer an online course, I continue to coach and mentor, and NEVER do I ever say or do the same thing twice. And NEVER are the outputs from those who go through the process ever the same. I will continue to iterate in perpetuity, so let's stay connected. Together, we can iterate the process and make it bigger and better! Share your learnings, and I will continue to share mine—together we can surely make the world a better place and live more fulfilled lives in the process!

While the digital world continues to expand and shift in a myriad of directions, I will always have a home base and **the door will always be open at www.nicolegallucci.com** where you will be able to find updates and places to share online and off. Join me and let me know how you are doing along the journey to living your best and fullest life.

Visit anytime!
I hope to see you soon!

Acknowledgments

Whoosh, I don't know where to start. This book is about life and a process for creating an extraordinary life. "It takes a village" and in my case it has taken a village, and it has been a wild, never-a-dull-moment journey. Thanking everyone that has gotten me to this point and has contributed to my life journey (positively and negatively), and therefore to the creating of the Life Blueprint process, is a book in itself! So I am going to keep it brief.

Thank you to my book team. To the Soul Seed Legacy publishing team and specifically Sabrina Greer, who from the moment we connected made me feel like my book was worthy. To Kelly Lamb, who gently edited and inspired. To Michelle Fairbanks, who brought the book to visual life, which was so important to me given the very nature of the contents and the intimacy of the work done by the reader as they go through the process. To Christine Stock, who at the end ensured everything came together seamlessly. To all of you for your patience, kindness, and respect for my vision for the book and my desire to have an impact.

To You, thank you for pulling up a chair. Thank you for engaging. Thank you for putting pen to paper or fingers to keyboard! To see this book in someone's hand as they walk past me will likely make me cry. If that is you, get ready for a hug because I will be coming in hot! I hope this book serves you. I hope it helps you live the life of your dreams and the life you deserve.

To my three, I will close the book the same way I opened it—you three are the greatest loves of my life and my unequivocal reason for being.

EXTRAORDINARY blessings to all.

XO Nicole

Templates, Suggested Reading, and Other Things of Interest

The QR code that was noted several times throughout the book is below. It will lead you to copies of all of the charts that you can download, print, and use with ease. I HIGHLY recommend you do this!

It will also lead you to my website and social platforms where I share all the things rambling around in my mind and my life. You might find them interesting. They may make you smile or laugh or think. Enjoy!

Contact Page

You can find me here 24/7:
On Instagram: nicole_gallucci
Via email: nicole@nicolegallucci.com

Want more?

You can find the latest and greatest
musings of my mind,
books that are inspiring me,
music that is speaking to my soul,
and meditations that are enlightening at
www.nicolegallucci.com

SOUL SEED
LEGACY · HOUSE

At Soul Seed Legacy House, we help thought leaders and creative entrepreneurs capture their vision in the form of nonfiction books, journals, workbooks, affirmation cards, and personal growth products.

Our mission is to help our authors grow and scale a platform far beyond the book, protect their soul's work, and turn their message into a legacy!

www.sslegacyhouse.com

 @sslegacyhouse

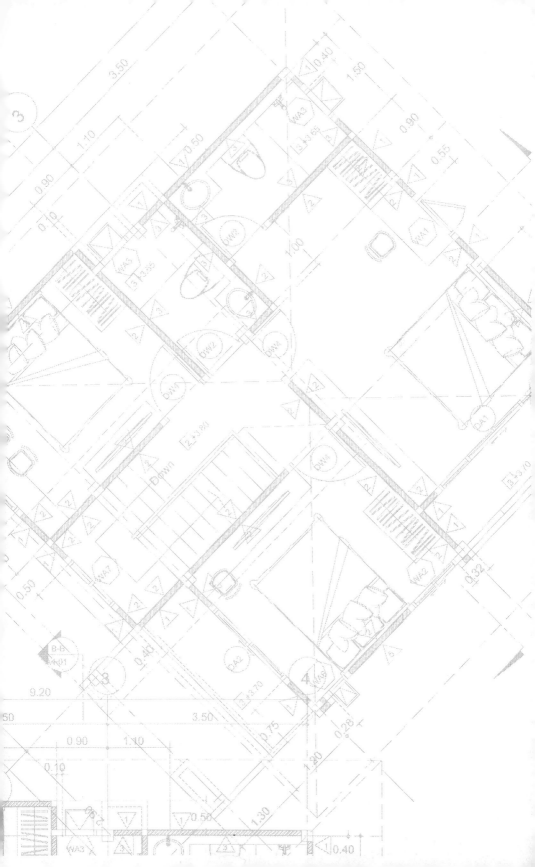

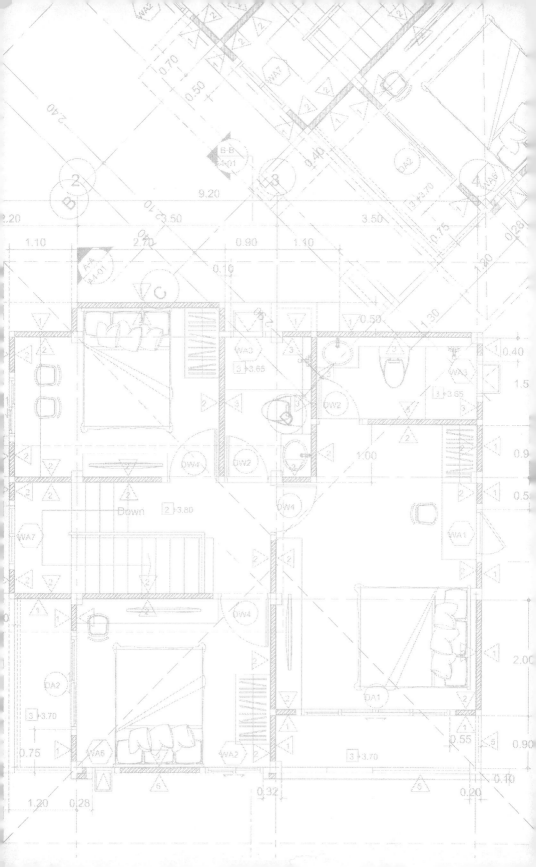

Manufactured by Amazon.ca
Bolton, ON

36396329R00118